EDUCATION, PEACE AND DEVELOPMENT

EDUCATION, PEACE AND DEVELOPMENT

Edited by

Dr. Ravindra Kumar

KALPAZ

Education, Peace and Development

ISBN: 978-81-7835-932-8

Published in 2012 in India by
Kalpaz Publications
C-30, Satyawati Nagar Delhi-110052
E mail: kalpaz@hotmail.com
Laser type setting: Dinesh Kumar
Printed at: Chawla Offset Printers, Delhi

Contents

PART- 4: METHODOLOGY

PART- 5: CASE STUDIES

Foreword

The Indian belief is that knowledge leads to the realization of self. Other effects are mere information. Compiiation or collection of information is not knowledge. Knowledge gives insight. The realized man is a seer, a *kavi* [poet], who has the power to enter the shell, the cover, and see the hidden truth. The modern man, as is found all over the world today, is bombarded every moment with new information through the internet. Printed matters also add endless information, but do not add knowledge. There is no light, only heat, no vision, only noise.

It proves the failure of the prevailing system of education in the world. Modern technology has provided all-round material prosperity, huge wealth and amenities, but not peace. Violence and terrorism, struggles and wars have made man sleepless. Where is peace? It has become elusive. It seems so near, but yet so far, beyond the reach of modern man. The truth is that no university, no country, no government have planned and worked for peace. They talk ceaselessly about peace, but in fact they always drift away from it.

The UNO, with its several arms, as laid down in its charter, is entrusted to ensure peace in the world. But the Organization itself is not a representative body. It has five permanent members who enjoys all the powers and who always use the Veto power even to the smallest reform. This body, from its very birth, has functioned as a dictator that wants to fetch democracy to this world. Nonetheless, this is sought through its own ideology, which is often not to the choice of the people of the country where this democracy is thrust.

The UNO is slowly, but surely, turning into a conglomeration that has forgotten its charter, lost its way and is now imposing its wish, will and order for furthering the vested interests of its powerful permanent members, who have little respect for the opinion of the global people, their needs and their aspirations. These powerful members, with their growing power of modern technology, use or abuse, misinform and misguide, the people and hence create conditions conducive for peace. If based on real education and real development, they rather block the very road, which leads to the cherished goal of world peace. Too often they side with the oppressors and thus dehumanize human beings living in their native states, in their traditional societies, and may be their traditional life styles.

Development, and modernization, or both, have now mainly become tools of economic exploitation for those who want to create new markets, areas of exploitation of natural resources, oil and other minerals in particular. Nevertheless, the claim is a *civilizing mission* or another sound bite. Due to their prejudices all the world powers have fixed views on world problems. It is often said that it is an age of science and technology. However, this is nothing but a misnomer. Science still mentally lives in the age of Newton whose worldviews was dualistic. For Newton the world consisted of the two basic elements –water and energy. His theory of gravity enunciates the law of power of gravitation of mass. It was the law of three-dimensional world. This law was modified by Einstein, which added the fourth dimension – the factor of time. This led us to the space-time continuum. Einstein's theory of 1905 was proved to be correct in 1919 by eminent British astronomers like Sir Arthur Eddington and Sir James Jeans. But, who cares for truth even in the world of science?

Big powers want other nations to talk to yet others for the resolution of conflict. But, they themselves have never done so. Only Russia and China have been the exception. After a series of long drawn negotiations both were able to resolve their conflicts. Now, they have no border dispute. What about the other nations in a similar predicament? Have they followed this path?

For the resolution of any conflict one will have to go to the origin of the conflict and the reasons for that. But, few are prepared to take pains for that. For example, Narendra Singh Sarila's book, *The Shadow of the Great Game: The Untold Story of India's Partition* has almost gone unnoticed. Even Indian leaders, policymakers and diplomats have not read it, just have seen it, but they claim that they are trying to resolve the conflict! Is it not the most amazing game?

India won freedom under the leadership of Mahatma Gandhi. He was the man, who ended the Euro-American Empire over the world. We are yet to reconcile this new situation, the changing of hands in a non-violent way and the emergence of a vibrating socio-economic-political democracy, instead of the mere political democracy style of Euro-Americans. But, as he had warned this was not enough. If private capitalism is replaced by state capitalism, or the White Sahib is replaced by the Black Sahib the conflict is not going to be resolved. They are all models of a *pyramidal structural system*. What Gandhiji suggested was an *Oceanic Structural System*.

The Last Will and Testament, written by the Mahatma on the day before his assassination is supposed to be a supplement to his seminal book *Hind Swarajya*, which needs to be read time and again today in this war-torn, crisis-ridden world. Anthony J Parel writes, ***"Gandhi's last political message is that in a free society political parties must be inspired by the ideal that politics is a form of public service rather than the means of dominating fellow citizens."*** The last word in the physical science is Einstein's $E=mc^2$; the last word in the spiritual science is the *Rigvedic Mantra* [1: 164: 46]. The Truth is one, but the sages call it by different names; the last word in the social science is Gandhi's *Satyagraha*. The reconciliation of the trio is the solution of the conflicts of the modern world, which is at the brink of the unprecedented depression leading to worldwide chaos and dehumanization of the whole system.

Another very obvious fact is often forgotten. For Gandhiji non-violence was the means and the end was to realize truth. No doubt, he attached great importance to purity of means. Nevertheless end is end and means is means. Pure means leads to pure destination. Everybody should be pure, but is not. Everybody can aspire to be pure and thus, slowly but steadily, can achieve the goal.

Let us keep in mind that he wrote, *The Story of My Experiments with Truth*. He did not name it *The Story of My Experiments with Non-violence*. You may wonder why I am laying so much stress on this fact. Today, in the name of non-violence, truth is being fudged. Naturally, if the mouth is shut, if all doors for conversation, communication and conflict resolution are shut, it will explode in violent expression, in the forms of armed conflicts and in extreme case, terrorism.

Truth is God. Gandhiji lived and died for it. He died for truth. But is he dead? The body is not there, but the light is there. *The Time*, in its December issue [last week of 1999] termed Gandhi and Einstein as the two greatest men of this millennium. It is a half-hearted tribute. They were the greatest men in human history. They changed the course of history. They were humble and never made such claim. Their descendents did not spend vast monetary resources to erect any memorial or monument for them. Time is the killer, time is the healer and time is the keeper. Time will keep their flames burning, eternally like the stars in the heaven. Their flame is the eternal light house for them who have eyes to see.

This book gives us such eye-sight:

Twinkle-Twinkle Twins Star! World will wonder who are you!!

Dr. Ravindra Kumar, the editor of this volume entitled, *Education, Peace and Development*, is an eminent scholar. He has written and edited several books. He has been a good teacher and a successful Vice-Chancellor. He has been invited by various institutions and organizations in India and other countries to speak on peace and conflict reconciliation of which he is a renowned expert and has been editing a reputed journal on this subject.

The twelve people have also contributed for this volume on subjects of their specialization. Their essays will give rich food to satisfy their intellectual need on various subjects. It is a book, which I believe, will be equally popular in scholars, students as well as common readers.

India is the only multi-racial, multi-cultural, multi-lingual and multi-layered democracy in the world, besides being the greater vibrating democracy. Future of democracy, in India as well as in other parts of the world, depends upon the maturity of citizens who are able to resolve their conflicts by their own initiatives. Hitherto Indian democracy has stood the test of time. Now globalization, along with nuclear weaponization, has new challenges. This book gives tips for those who are trying to find the way out of this depressing darkness.

Prof. Siddheshwar Prasad

Introduction

Education is the means for an all-round development of man. Therefore, it is needless to mention its role and importance in human life. Mahatma Gandhi noted, ***"Education is an unending exercise till death. Only it can act as a means to the end of a successful life. It can help mould and shape human body, mind and character in such a manner that they may act as means to achieve joys and efficiency."***

Peace and development are subjects of human life, which, apart from connecting to one-another are necessary elements that make life purposeful. Moreover, if both –peace and development– are defined and analyzed separately, it will become apparent that they are dynamic in their nature and complementary to one-another.

Further, to create an atmosphere of peace, to guide people on the true pathway to development, the role of education is vital. As argued earlier, education is the only means for the all-round development of man. Moreover, as the Mahatma rightly observes, it is a lifelong process that guides mankind. Therefore, to set forth the argument that education, besides becoming a concrete source of guidance to transform life to one of peaceful existence, is also a concrete means and medium to attain progress at all levels and in all walks of life, is justified.

Thus, we can see education, peace and development as inter connected aspects of human life; they cannot be separated from one-another and their role cannot be minimized. The significance of all these three aspects in human life is brought together in this volume entitled, *Education, Peace and Development.*

In this volume the contributors, scholars from India and abroad, have, by accepting the importance of the subject, attempted to present their respective viewpoints on the topics of education, peace and development. Divided into five parts –General Observation, Gandhian Perspectives, Conflict Resolution, Overview and Case Studies– this volume is an attempt to draw the attention of those interested in the subject besides the general reader.

I am thankful to Dr. Geeta Mehta, Mr. Suleman Kakar, Dr. Lokanath Mishra, Mr. Ram Puniyani, Professor Rachana Chakraborty, Dr. Preeti Sharma, Dr. Sanjeev Kumar, Professor Vibhuti Patel, Ms. Chandrika De Alwis, Ms. Patricia Hess, Professor Enver Duran, Ms. Fatma Ozkan, Ms. Sema Duran, Ms. Aslı Özen, Professor Hilmi Ibar and Dr. Handan Çelik for their valuable contributions, and to Professor Siddheshwar Prasad for contributing a foreword to this volume.

Ravindra Kumar

Contributors

Aslı Ozen: Formerly a teacher at the Beykent College of Edirne and a known researcher in semiotics, linguistics, language acquisition, culture teaching and methodology, is currently the LLP/Erasmus at the Trakya University, Turkey.

Chandrika De Alwis: A renowned research scholar from Sri Lanka, who for years has been working in the diverse fields of international relations, consultancy in public relations, media communication and education. A known figure researching conflict reporting, freedom of expression and conflict resolution, she, besides participating in many international conferences, has published articles in various national and international journals and currently is a member of the Asia Media Information Centre and the Asia Pacific Peace Research Association.

Enver Duran: Presently the rector of the Trakya University, Turkey has worked as an intern doctor in the Gulhane Medical Military Academy and a specialist in the Thoracic-Cardiovascular Surgery in the same Academy in 1980; has worked as the Clinic Director of Cardiovascular Surgery, Gulhane Military Medical Academy, Haydarpasha Training and Application Hospital from 1990 to 1998 and as the Chairman of the

Trakya University Department of Cardiovascular Surgery since 2004; is a member of many organizations including Thrombosis, Homeostasis and Angelology Society of Turkey, the European Society for Vascular Surgery, the Turkish Society of Cardiovascular Surgery, the National Association of Phlebology and the Turkish Society of Cardiology.

Geeta Mehta: A retired head of the department of philosophy from Maharshri Dayanand College, is presently the director of KJ Somaiya Centre for Studies in Jainism; is the author of three known books: *Philosophy of Vinoba Bhave: A New Perspective in Gandhian Thought*; *Aba [Shivaji Bhave] Apne Sabdonme*; and *Ahimsa From Mahavira to Mahatma;* besides, she has published dozens of papers in various national-international Journals.

Handan Celik: Currently an instructor of English at the Trakya University, Turkey is also associated with the international relations department of the same University; has been carrying out researches in the field of English language teaching, particularly EFL teacher education, professional development, second language acquisition, foreign language teaching methodology, and inter-language and developmental pragmatics.

Hilmi İbar: Currently a professor of chemistry in the department of analytical chemistry at the Trakya

University, has also been serving as a department chair and the dean of faculty of education and international relations; has been a student of the Aston University, Birmingham, and research scholar of the University of Missouri–Kansas City, USA; besides publishing many books, he has contributed a number of articles to the international journals of repute in analytical chemistry, inorganic and organic materials, environmental analyses and chromatography.

Loknath Mishra: A master degree holder in mathematics and education from the Saṃbalpur University, Orissa, India, is currently a principal at the Vivek College of Education, Bijnor, U. P.; has authored five books on subjects related to peace education. Besides organizing many national-international conferences on peace education, he has been editing the VIVEK journal of education for the last five years.

Muhammad Suleman Kakar: Currently the managing director of Cooperation for Peace and Unity [CPAU], Afghanistan, is a renowned peace builder and leader, a researcher, and a community development expert; has worked in many national and international NGOs besides holding key government positions; has served as the Deputy Minister of Education in the Islamic Republic of Afghanistan.

Patricia Hess: A master degree holder in interdisciplinary studies from Sul Ross State University in Alpine, Texas, USA, is a well-known scholar of psychology, social sciences, religion, sociology, anthropology and political science and a Korean teacher of English at the Kimpo College; has been a summer volunteer for Ameri Corps to assist elementary students, who were behind in their reading skills and developed activities to help them.

Preeti Sharma: Currently an associate professor and head of the department of history and Indian culture at Banasthali University, Rajasthan, India, she teaches ancient Indian history, social history of modern India, issues in modern world history, research methodology, and historiography at undergraduate and postgraduate levels. Her area of specialization is ancient Indian history, Indian art and architecture, and South Indian rock-cut art and architecture. Her areas of interest include gender studies, especially women's representation in art and literature, feminine sexuality, social history with special bearings on patriarchic formations, cultural formations, folk lore of Rajasthan, art studies, etc. She has published several research papers in reputed journals on related issues and has also successfully carried out a UGC project on South Indian rock-cut temple architecture. She is currently working on interpretations of Mahabalipuram relief as a UGC

Inter University Centre Research Associate in humanities and social sciences at the prestigious Indian Institute of Advanced Study, Rashtrapati Nivas, Shimla.

Rachana Chakraborty: Currently a professor of history in the University of Calcutta, West Bengal, India, engaged in research in history of education-administration and management of higher education in Bengal 1919-1947, women's education, employment and empowerment in colonial and post-colonial periods, caste studies; has authored, edited and contributed in books/journals, both national and international; participated in and chaired sessions at various international and national seminars viz. IAHA [Dhaka, Taipei], ICAS [Kuala Lampur], ATINER [Athens]; has received national level post-doctoral award from the University Grants Commission, Government of India.

Ram Puniyani: A former professor of IIT Mumbai, has been working for national integration, communal harmony and peace for the last two decades and has written extensively on issues pertaining to these topics for a fortnightly column on www.pluralindia.com and several other periodicals. He has published the books: *Second Assassination of Gandhi* [2002], *Communalism: Facts Versus Myths* [2003], *Terrorism: Facts versus Myths* [2007], and *Dalits: Social Justice* [2009], and has conducted workshops on these topics.

He is a recipient of Indira Gandhi National Integration Award [2006] and National Communal Harmony Award [2007].

Ravindra Kumar: An Indologist and a former vice chancellor of Meerut University, India, has authored and edited over 100 works on great personalities like Gautama Buddha and Mahatma Gandhi and on various social-cultural issues. As a visiting professor, scholar and guest speaker he has delivered hundreds of lectures on Asian values, Gandhism, international understanding and peace in many countries of the world. The editor of Global Peace International Journal since 2001, and author of *Theory and Practice of Gandhian Non-Violence* [2002], *Non-Violence and its Philosophy* [2003], *Towards Buddha* [2007] and *Gandhian Thoughts: New World, New Dimensions* [2008], he is a recipient of several awards like Ambassador of Peace, Sardar Patel Award and Padma Shri by the President of India.

Sanjeev Kumar H. M.: An assistant professor in the department of political science at the University of Allahabad, India, he teaches western political philosophy, political theory and international relations at undergraduatc and postgraduate levels, besides supervising doctoral research. His area of specialization is democratization in South Asia, India-Pakistan relations and Subcontinental security, and the role of the United States in Subcontinental politics. His areas of interest also include contemporary issues involving multiculturalism, globalization and the identity of Muslims, world order post-9/11, the role of political parties in the shaping of India's foreign policy, ethno-political conflict and conflict resolution in South Asia, and women's human rights. He has published extensively in these areas in journals of international and national repute, including the Economic and Political Weekly [EPW] and India Quarterly. Currently he is availing the prestigious UGC Inter University Centre's Research Associateship in humanities and social sciences at the Indian Institute of Advanced Study, Rashtrapati Nivas, Shimla.

Sema Duran: Currently a researcher at the department of classroom education, faculty of education, Trakya University, Turkey, and her major research areas include: linguistics, first language acquisition and language teaching methodology.

Vibhuti Patel: A professor and head of the university department of economics, and director of department of postgraduate studies and research of SNDT Women's University, Mumbai, who is a member of expert committee on School of Gandhian Thoughts and also a member of expert committee of school of gender and development studies for Indira Gandhi Open University [IGNOU], New Delhi together a member of subgroup on gender and agriculture for the Eleventh Five Year Plan, the Planning Commission of India. She is an expert committee member of Seventh Survey of Education Research and Advisory Board Member of Department of Women's Studies of NCERT, Delhi, India.

*****

Part 1
General Observation

1
Education for Peace

Geeta Mehta

Abstract: It is education, which has the potential to pass on or to transform the social, cultural, economic, and political values of the next generation. It can be said that each generation is the mirror of its educational system. Understandings of peace, social justice and moral values, and of their application to the real life of individuals, can be inculcated through education offered in schools and colleges. A teacher is a bridge between the past and the future. He has to bring about a peaceful, social transformation. The teachers should be ashamed that a police force has entered the university campuses. Teachers should deliberately plan to make police action unnecessary in the future. To attain a peaceful world, peace has to be constructed from below. Peace is not merely an absence of violence. It is something more since it is also a positive state of mind as well as a constructive goal of person, society and mankind. An urge for peace is seen in man's striving for harmony, wholeness, completeness in individual and social life by eliminating the areas of conflict and widening the areas of harmony. Peace is a state of harmony between parts and the whole. Humanity is striving to achieve harmony by undertaking constructive programmes. It is reflected in various activities such as the establishment of organizations like the UNO, UNESCO,

UNICEF, International Red Cross, Non- alignment Movement, The Green Peace Movement, Pacifist Movement, Amnesty International etc. Peace, which has its base in the existential truth of human life offers humanity a faith that kingdom of peace will be a reality one day, even though that day may be the remotest in the history of mankind.

Basic Meaning of Peace

The basic meaning of peace is a harmonious, socially adjustable and mutually cooperative peaceful life-style.

Peace as conceived in Indian context is concerned with *self-culture* or *self-development of each and every individual of the society with the emphasis on moral elevation.*

In particular, the expression of *Shanti* is the culmination of various features of Hindu, Jain and Buddhist traditions. It epitomizes peace of the mind, peace of the inner self, interpersonal peace. *Shanti* means *Ahimsa*, connotes love for human, sub-human world and nature. Further, it implies collective consciousness of people, functioning in a common assembly based on equality and integral unity of human beings. On the one hand, *Shanti* stresses individual self-restraint, sacrifice, service and compassion, on the other; it emphasizes morality, concern for human welfare backed by prayer and service.[1]

Peace in different Cultures

Historians all over the world have been more occupied with the stories of war while peace movements have been very significant from the very beginning of human culture. For example, in Judaic culture *Shalom* is a form of greeting for material prosperity, while in Arabic culture *Salam* expresses a wish for peace in interpersonal relationships; Greek tradition believes in *Irene* the Goddess of peace, who brings peace which leads to material well- being. *Pax* or Roman word for peace is still used for treaties or contract between two or more nations. In India *Shanti* has been a multifaceted concept and it has a considerable impact on Indian life style from the very beginning of her recorded history. The oldest literatures of *the Sanatana Dharma*, i.e., the *Vedas* have many *Shanti mantras*, which form the beginning as well as end of each *Upanishad*. Every *Upanishad* starts with *Shanti mantra* and also ends with *Shanti mantras*. This shows the keenness of the people for peace in the world.

The emerging global ethic, therefore, demands that history of human culture must be understood from the point of view of peace-movements and efforts.

Although the origins of peace education are as ancient as humankind itself, only in this century with its two world wars has the subject become a systematic focus of attention. The first nuclear bomb used against Japan and the threat of nuclear weapons have been turning points in the field of peace education. That is why peace education began first in the United States, Canada, some European countries, and Japan.

Peace is Striving for Harmony

An urge for peace is seen in man's striving for harmony, wholeness, completeness in individual and social life by eliminating the areas of conflict and widening the areas of harmony. The urge for peace in terms of harmony is one of the truths of human life. It will therefore continue to govern human life as long as the nature of human life continues to be the same. This urge is both realistic and idealistic.

It may be said that peace is a bipolar state referring to the actual and potential-ideal state of human life. Man's yearning and striving for peace has a rock bottom foundation on this existential truth of human life, and therefore peace lovers cannot be said to be living in a world of utopia or dreams, which can never be translated into reality.

Peace at Individual and Social Level

Peace has both individual and social aspects, micro as well as macro aspects. Peace at the individual level is the inner peace or peace of mind, a state in which there is perfect harmony among the various psychic forces which otherwise pull in different directions and become a source of conflict and tension. It is a psychological state when mind is free from tension, stress and strain, the different passions and desires and the conflicts that arise from them. It thus signifies a tranquil composure, a peacefulness of temper. At the individual level, it indicates a state in which the sense of being full or complete is experienced when all the faculties of an individual are in full harmony or in total, orderly alliance with one another.

At the social level it indicates a harmonious community as peace is the natural or moral condition of man in relationship to others enjoined most intimately in the family, and extended to others by a societal bond. Social peace is a state of harmonious relationship between individual as well as groups with varied interests. It is a state in which there is absence of conflicts and presence of cooperation in spite of differences.

It is a state of harmony between parts and the whole.

They saw the integral relationship between the individual and the society, the microcosm and the macrocosm, and held that the peace of the individual and that of the society were not merely inter-dependent, but the path to peace was identical for both the individual and the society.

Peace at Micro and Macro Levels

All the great religions of the world have an emphasis on values such as observing truth in thought, words and deeds, living a life of self-restraint, having active love for others etc. It is necessary for man to develop altruistic qualities, which are essential for the promotion of peace as they help in developing a sense of solidarity and identity of interests.

Unless we are able at least intellectually to comprehend this inner spiritual link that binds the whole human race into a single family, cutting across all barriers of nationality or religions, caste or creed, sex or social status, we will not be able to establish ourselves in the inner peace.

All religions preach peace, but in fact religion has been one of the major sources of violent conflict down through the centuries, and remains so even today, science was supposed to help establish peace, but it has created increasingly deadly weapons of mass destruction.

Education for Peace

Peace is a process of progress of socio- economic justice, mutual respect, and equality of human rights to food, shelter, education, health, and political participation among the peoples. In brief, in the words of Naidu, it is ***"the opportunity for self-***

actualization which is the highest level of human needs."[2]

In short, education for peace and justice in the words of Joseph J Fahey, "***is academic in nature, multi-disciplinary in method, global in perspective, and oriented toward action that is intelligent constructive, and creative.***"[3]

Peace education includes a wide range of subjects. They may include any or all of the following:

- War [its causes and results], armament control and disarmament, dangers of nuclearization of weapons and industries;
- Negative consequences of militarization in terms of economics, politics and psychology;
- Harmful consequences of ecological destruction;
- Evils of colonialism;
- Inhumanity of structural violence such as the deprivation of the basic necessities of life [food, shelter, clothing, medical care, and education], the denial of political freedoms and rights that usually determine all other aspects of life;
- Social justice, social change, and economic welfare;
- Philosophy and methodology of non-violence;
- Crisis of industrialization and; developmentalism; and
- The helpful roles of some international organizations.[4]

The purpose of peace education, according to Reardon, is "***to provide knowledge and skills, as well as capacities and commitment, to overcome obstacles to peace, and to build a global community, which encompasses the entire human family and accords equal value and full dignity to all human beings.***"[5] Another peace educator, TB Monez describes the purpose of peace education in this way, "***Its***

basic purpose is to help students design strategies of action, which can contribute to the shaping of a world order characterized by social justice and absence of exploitation."[6]

The Possibility of Education for Peace and Justice

Although religion on the one hand, can be used to sanction war or conflicts within and among the nations, on the other hand, it offers positive goals for peace and justice. All the great world religions promote justice, love of humanity, human cooperation and therefore, peace for both individuals and for society. If the believers of these religions follow just the golden rules of their respective faiths, many social problems faced today would be solved; and wars and conflicts within and among the nations would be reduced. As RS Johnson points out, ***"Religion offers no short-term solution, no palliative or panacea for the world's ills likely to find an immediate application. But unquestionably religion offers to men the only final solution of the world's problems, but it is a long term solution."***[7]

Some scholars and philosophers in the West are very optimistic about stopping wars. For instance, the well-known philosopher, Bertrand Russell, argued that ***"If the world could live for a few generations without war, war would soon come to seem as absurd dueling has come to seem to us. No doubt there would still be some homicidal maniacs, but they would no longer be heads of Governments."***[8]

John Huddleston is more hopeful about stopping war. He writes, ***"Just as in the nineteenth century it was possible, by a combination of consciousness raising and legislation***

***to bring about the voluntary abolition of the institution of slavery though several thousand years old. So too it is possible to abolish the scourge of war by the end of this millennium if there is a will to do so."*[9]**

It is education, which has the potential to pass on or to transform the social, cultural, economic and political values of the next generation. It can be said that each generation is the mirror of its educational system. The understandings of peace, social justice and moral values, and of their application to the real life of individuals can be inculcated through education offered in schools.[10]

Teaching Methods

In order to teach peace education effectively, we must give importance to at least four points: First, peace education must be academic in nature. It must be based on an academic discipline having its own research methods and contents. Second, instead of using only one method, as many methods as possible must be used integrating resources from different disciplines such as history, sociology, psychology, economy, politics, and religion. Peace education is by nature interdisciplinary. Third, it must be studied globally. Today wars and conflicts, arm races, and international trade and finance link many nations and countries. Thus, when we study peace education, we must always consider its international dimensions. Finally, peace education requires not only theoretical studies, but also action. This is a most important point concerning peace education. If we do not try to stop wars, conflicts, excessive military expenditures and socioeconomic injustices prevailing in society, what is the point of studying about them? If we want peace and justice, we must prepare for peace and justice. This means, in the words of Krieger and Kelly, ***"Education for peace and building and strengthening institutions at the regional and global levels that will be capable of supporting and maintaining peace."***[11]

Teacher's Role in Peace Education

Role of a teacher is very important in the process of imparting education. He should explain the facts effectively and objectively and try to inspire the students to inculcate among themselves creative and constructive thinking. The young creative mind of the student is more amenable to become constructive when chiseled by the factual information provided by the teacher. In the words of Martin Luther King Junior, ***'We have guided missiles and misguided men."***

Education, for Mahatma Gandhi, is an instrument of socio-economic progress and moral development. Formal literacy for him did not constitute real education. It is neither the end of education nor the beginning. It is only one of the means whereby men and women can be educated.[12]

True education, according Gandhi, consists of an all-round drawing out of the best in child and man, body, mind and spirit.[13] His main emphasis is on the three H's, i.e., head, heart and hand, rather than on the three R's, i.e., reading, writing and arithmetic.[14] He laid equal stress on the education of heart, i.e., refinement of emotions and impulses and awakening of deepest feelings of love, sympathy and friendship.[15]

It is a life-long process. It should cultivate the spirit of toleration, cooperation, public sprit and a sense of responsibility.[16]

It will be obvious that education that insists on the promotion of values as a part of the development of personality demands from the teacher a new role. This role demands from the teacher subtler dimensions. Another trinity of qualities that can be mentioned is that of purity, patience and perseverance, which are indispensable in surmounting any weakness or limitation of our nature. And, finally, we may note the trinity of calm, profundity and intensity, which open the doors to an ever progressive search of perfection.[17]

Gandhian Way of Peace–Education

To attain a peaceful world, Peace has to be constructed from below. To ensure a peaceful world, societies or states constituting the world order must themselves be peaceful or peace-loving, peaceful societies in their turn must be ones based on peaceful constituent parts, peace cannot be imposed from above.

Peace can be constructed only through peaceful and just means. Gandhian concept of *Ahimsa* and *Satyagraha,* Buddha's *Samyak Ajivika* [correct living] or Christ's concept of love can be the effective means to build up peaceful societies. Only such peaceful societies as integral parts can ensure a peaceful world order.

Out of seven social sins according to Gandhi, the fourth dictum "***knowledge without character***", deals with knowledge. Gandhi's system of ***Basic Education*** was a system for development of justice in society. True knowledge leads to the development of justice in society where one evolves his rational self. Gandhi States, ***"The truest test of civilization, culture and dignity is character and not clothing."***[18]

Gandhi could perceive the need for a coordinated human being, not coordinated merely in body, mind, feeling, and soul, but coordinated with his fellow human beings. Education according to Gandhi should aim at producing not only good individuals, but socially useful citizens who understand their social responsibilities as an integral element of society.[19]

Global Perception on Peace Education

Gandhi writes, ***"Things of fundamental to the people are not secured by reason alone, but have to be purchased with their suffering... if you want something really important to be done, you must not merely satisfy the reason, you must move the heart also. The appeal of reason is more to the head, but the penetration of the heart comes from suffering. It opens up the inner understanding of man."***[20]

To put it in a nutshell, if we want to do a better job of training people of reducing wars, violence and killing, we must ***"add Gandhi to Galtung"***, i.e., train and stimulate individual people to act in non-violent ways appropriate tc the situation. Gandhi says, ***"Every religion that I know of, lays the responsibility for a better life on this earth on the individual: peace must begin with me not the government, the clergy, or the heavens."***

In an article on, adding Gandhi to Galtung for peace work, Theodore Herman writes, Gandhi made at least four contributions to individual peace work that are worth incorporating into our own Western peace research and education programmes:

- A principled or ethical emphasis on the link between means and ends that guided his whole life;
- Constant testing of beliefs by one's own actions;
- The steady growth or transformation from personal views to a wider world view of peace; and
- The constant use of publicity as to motives and actions.

"I have a faith that a day will come when the world will come to India in search for peace and India and Asia will become the light of the world", said M. K. Gandhi to Egyptian delegates to the Asian conference on April 4, 1947.

The time has not yet come to remake man in tune with the increasing command he has acquired over nature through science and technology. When that time comes, Gandhi and the universals of Indian culture may once again acquire relevance.

Integral Relationship of Peace

True to his belief in the integral relationship of the peace of the individual and that of the society, Mahatma Gandhi prescribed a code of conduct consisting of eleven vows for disciplining the mind of the individual towards peace and non-violence and an eighteen-point constructive programme for the transformation of the society.

In integral philosophy of Gandhiji, each and every field is connected with the other. He says, ***"If the recognized leaders of mankind, who have control over the engines of destruction, were wholly to renounce their use, with full knowledge of its implications, permanent peace can be obtained."***

As peace is one of the values amongst the cluster of values

such as truth, justice, freedom, equality, brotherhood, human dignity, love etc. a peaceful social structure reflects a harmony in human interrelationship in terms of these values. If it deviates from any of these values, it becomes less peaceful to that extent. It may further be observed that no social structure can be described as a peaceful structure except in terms of its operative social function.

A non-violent social structure can be said to be a peaceful social structure as it is non-exploitative, egalitarian and encourages social interrelationship, which is free from greed, inequality, injustice etc.

According to Gandhi, education should teach importance of physical labour and should be helpful in character building of the student. He wanted a person to be self-reliant and having self- control by observing the eleven vows, which he practiced and preached. Such a kind of education if propagated will have the citizens of higher spotless character.

Work and knowledge must never be separated what we need today is working minds and thinking fingers- mingling of knowledge and work.

Work develops intelligence and intelligence adds efficiency to work. Therefore, mutual cooperation of the intelligentsia and the proletariat is indispensable for the perfection of society. This will be the basis of equality. Keeping this objective in view, the basic education scheme has adopted the principle of education through industry.

Gandhi's system of education desired to develop three aspects of the individual the mind, the heart and the skill to use his hands. The child knows with his mind, loves with his heart and creates with his hands. Unless we provide outlets for all three and training in all three areas, the child has lopsided education. We need rethinking about *specialization.* Too much emphasis on *specialization* has weakened the spirit of integration and social commitment. Basic education conceives a society in which people will have an understanding of their duties and responsibilities and will habitually fulfill them. They will possess the spirit of love and cooperation. They will cultivate the virtue of self-dependence through labour. There will be coordination in their economic, social and political activities, which will be firmly based on national industries, agriculture and other co-operative industries. In other words, basic education teaches man the art of living, which binds heart to heart and yields spiritual pleasure. Basic education is not merely the art, which teaches how to earn money. In the craze to earn money man accumulates lifeless objects only and misses the precious gem of life.

While the external man has grown the internal man remains neglected. The resulting crisis demands, therefore, the development of the inner man and organized integrating of the internal and external man. If education has to become an instrument of meeting this crisis, its aim should be to cultivate, sharpen and transform the faculties and powers of personality leading towards their increasing integration and perfection.

Stable peace cannot be nurtured merely because man's economic or social rights are secured, as he also needs intellectual liberty and growth and opportunity to develop his creative ability. What man needs is a positive, creative and dynamic peace of harmonious relationships coupled with creative joy and satisfaction of his basic instincts. So the eighteen points constructive programme promoted by Gandhiji is relevant here. An Integrated approach as suggested by Gandhiji based on the reformation of the individual by giving him the required training and self-discipline, side by side with reconstruction of society through non-violent means, may pave the way for societal peace.

Striving for Peace

Humanity is striving to achieve harmony by undertaking constructive programmes. It is reflected in various activities such as the establishment of organizations like the UNO, the UNESCO, the UNICEF, the International Red Cross, the Non-align Movement, The Green Peace Movement, the Pacifist Movement, the Amnesty International etc.

Gandhi said, ***"I have no doubt that unless big nations shed their desire of exploitation and the spirit of violence of which war is the natural expression and atom bomb the inevitable consequence, there is no scope for peace in the world."***[21]

More and more nations should be persuaded to join the Non-aligned Movement and follow an independent policy of their own. Also, the principle of ***Panchasheel*** should be accepted as guidelines by all nations for international relations.

Efforts should be made in direction of disarmament. Even American President Kennedy has pointed out that the risks of disarmament are much less than those of the arms race.[22]

Only Department of peace studies will not serve the

purpose. An international Institute can be established under the UNO or outside it to give special peace oriented training to diplomats of all countries. It is desirable to have, in each nation, a separate ministry in charge of promotion of peace, on par with the ministry of defense or external affairs. Education for excellence and culture of peace is a constitutional imperative.

Pre-requisite for World Peace

Vinoba states poetically that Peace can be built only on trust, not on mutual distrust.

"Vedanto vijnanam visvasah ceti saktyah tisrah|
Yasam sthairye nityam santih samrddhi bhavisyato jagati"[23]

[There are three powers- spirituality, science and trust-if they are stabilized in the world, then there will be peace and prosperity].

Peace will not be established among men unless men thirst for peace for its own sake. Peace will not come and the world will not be free from violence, until society knows and experiences the greatness and importance of the independent power of peace. Peace to be peace in the real sense of the term must be based on a genuine change of heart, when mutual distrust, hatred and enmity must ceasc for good, giving place to ever abiding friendship.

Peace is unattained by part performance of conditions, even as a chemical combination is impossible without complete fulfillment of the conditions of the attainment thereof.

References:

1. Vyas, Ramnarayan. 1966. *Peace Philosophy and Progress*. Delhi [India]: Sterling Publishers Ltd., page 33

2. Koylu, Mustafa. 2003. *Islam and its Quest for Peace*, page 120. Quoted from *Jihad, Justice and Education* by Naidu MV, Washington [USA]: The Council for Research in Values and Philosophy.

3. Fahey, Joseph J. 1986. *The Nature and Challenge of the Justice and Peace Education*, page 3 in *Justice and Peace Education: Models for College and University Faculty* by David M. Johnson [ed.]. Mory Knoll, NY [USA]: Orbis Books.

4. Monez, Thotnton B [ed.]. 1973. *Working For Peace, Focus on Mankind.* Washington [USA]: Book Committee ASCD.

5. Reardon, Betty A. 1982. *Militarization, Security and Peace Education,* pp. 39-40. UNME [USA]: Walley Forge.

6. Monez, Thormton B. 1973. *Peace: In Implications for Education: Working for Peace*, page 18. Washington DC ASCD [USA]: Book Committee.

7. Johnson, RC. 1970. *The Influence of Religions Teaching as a Factor in Maintaining Peace in Paths to Peace: A Study of War, Its Causes and Prevention*, page 349. New York [USA]: Books For Libraries Press.

8. Russell, Bertrand. 1961. Has Man a Future? page 51. London: George Allen and Unwin.

9. Huddleston, John. 1992. *Achieving Peace by the Year 2000: A Twelve Point Proposal*, page 90. Oxford [UK], Chatham and New York [USA]: One world.

10. Ibid, page 137

11. Krieger David and Frank K. Kelly [ed.]. 1937, July 31. *Introduction: In Waging Peace II: Vision and Hope for the Twenty-First Century*. Chicago [USA]: Noble Press.

12. Ibid

13. Patel, MS. 1953. *The Educational Philosophy of Mahatma Gandhi*, page 32. Ahmedabad [India]: Navajivan Publishing House.

14. Prabhu, RK and Rao, UR [eds.]. 1946. *The Mind of Mahatma Gandhi*, pp. 378-9. Ahmedabad [India]: Navajivan Publishing House.

15. Kabir, Humayun. 1961. *Education in New India*, page 23. London [UK]: George Allen and Unwin Ltd.

16. Joshi, Kireet. 1962. *Education and Character Building*, page 49, quoted in MC Dubey book *Basic Education and the New Social Order*. New Delhi [India]: National Council of Education, Research and Training.

17. Gandhi, MK. *The Collected Works of Mahatma Gandhi* [Volume XXXVI], page 258. New Delhi [India]: Publications Division.

18. Patel, VT. 1982, September. *Gandhi's Concept of Education*, in *Gandhi Marg* [Volume 6], pp-91-2. New Delhi [India]: Gandhi Peace Foundation.

19. Gandhi, MK. 1994. *All Men Are Brothers*, pp. 82-3. New York [USA]: Continuum.

20. Gandhi, MK [ed.]. 1946, November 10. *Harijan* Weekly. Ahmedabad [India]: Navajivan and RK Prabhu and UR Rao [eds.]. 1967. *The Mind of Mahatma Gandhi*, page 450. Ahmedabad [India]: Navajivan Publishing House.

21. Fernandez, Angelo. 1981. *Towards Peace with Justice*, page 17. New Delhi [India]: Indian Social Institute.

22. Bhave, Vinoba. 1985, November. *Maitri* [a Hindi Monthly], page 56. The Verse was originally composed on August 8, 1959

23. Message to Cosmopolitan, New York [USA] quoted in *Harijan* May 16, 1936. Also in *The Mind of Mahatma Gandhi*, page 455 by RK Prabhu and UR Rao, Ahmedabad [India]: Navajivan Publishing House.

*****

2

Five Points to Promote Peace through Education

Muhammad Suleman Kakar

Abstract: The context in which we are born and brought up sufficiently influences our attitude and behavior. Each of us is born male or female and born into a particular way of life: for example a nomad in a rural area of Asia or Africa and a citizen in Europe have radically different experience of life and things around them. We each have different sets of values, which guide our thinking and behavior. These values influence us to take certain actions and reject others. This reality of life in fact leads us to a situation where we find people who have different perspective on life and things when we meet them or work with them. In which case, conflict happens when people pursue different perspectives and goals that clash. In order to move a conflict habituated system to a peace system, we will need to change the way we think. The preamble of the Charter of the United Nations Educational, Social and Cultural Organization [UNESCO] echoes this sentiment, ***"since war begins in the minds of men, it is in the minds of men that the foundation of peace must be constructed."*** Change in the attitude and behavior can be achieved through formal or informal peace education.

Introduction

As we all know, peace seems to be humanity's fondest dream. Almost everyone claims to be in favor of peace, but it can be used to mean many different things. A situation that is peaceful for one group may be oppressive for another. When we think of peace, we often tend to think of war or violent conflict as it's opposite.

Scholars around the world define peace as the existence of peaceful relationships, active association and planned cooperation among persons and groups for achieving greater aims such as justice, security, and constructive transformation of conflicts.

Many people understand peace to be the absence of war. While, this is of course vital, others see it as only first step towards a fuller ideal, using definitions such as: an interweaving of relationships between individuals, groups and institutions that value diversity and foster the full development of human potential.

According to Galtung, peace has two dimensions ***'negative peace'*** and ***'positive peace'.***

Negative peace can be described as the absence of war or violent conflict [often the agreement between elites] as a static state. Other violence can continue e.g. cultural and structural violence. Positive peace is a dynamic process rather than an end state and implies a condition where conflicts are addressed and solved.

Along the same line, UNICEF, describes positive peace as a situation characterized not only by the absence of war or violent conflict, but also by presence of factors that reduce the likelihood of violent conflicts and promotes a better quality of life for all. These factors include social and economic justice, inter-group understanding, ecological balance, and opportunities for democratic participation in decision-making.

Mayor, an another scholar, explains that instead of the absence of war, peace is increasingly seen as a dynamic, participative, long-term process, based on universal values and everyday practice at all levels – the family, the school, the community, as well as the nation.

Others scholars have rather a greater view about peace. They define peace as an absence of all types of violence: ***physical violence, structural violence and cultural violence.*** According to this understanding, absence of physical violence alone is described as negative peace while absence of all three types of violence is described as positive peace. Physical violence is more visible while structural and cultural violence is less visible.

This understanding of positive peace draws the attention to the fact that it is an ultimate vision that individuals as well as groups and nations should pursue to achieve. It is quite understandable that in today's world the complete elimination of all three types of violence seems impossible. However, through sustained efforts by individuals, groups and institutions it is possible to reduce violence at all levels. Therefore, it is a whole life struggle and all of us must make the commitment to work for true peace and justice.

According to The Institute for Multi-Track Diplomacy, social peace building deals with feelings, attitude, opinions, beliefs, values, and skills as they are held and shared between peoples, individually and in groups. It is about building a human infrastructure of people who are committed to engendering a new culture, a *peace culture*, within the social fabric of communal and inter-communal life.

As a matter of fact, the context in which we are born and brought up sufficiently influences our attitude and behavior. Each of us is born male or female and born into a particular way of life: for example a nomad in a rural area of Asia or Africa and a citizen in Europe have radically different experience of life and things around them.

We each have different sets of values, which guide our thinking and behavior. These values influence us to take certain actions and reject others. This reality of life in fact leads us to a situation where we find people who have different perspectives on life and things when we meet them or work with them. In which case, conflict happens when people pursue different perspectives and goals that clash.

We find conflicts between ourselves and others in our families and communities; interpersonal conflict, when we find differences or perceived differences among our resources, needs, values, or interest. There is conflict found among the nations of the world, international conflicts, where again there is a difference or perceived difference between resources, needs and values or interests.

Conflict can be defined in a number of ways e.g. controversy, disagreements, disputes, struggle, fight, war and so on. Conflict is positive as well as negative. It is negative in the sense when it becomes destructive due to inability of the people to deal with it effectively. It is positive in the sense when it is used for growth, progress, and positive change. When we tend to define or understand conflict as a struggle between opposing forces or war, the negative connotations of this definition encourage us to avoid conflicts at any cost. However, if we view conflict as an opportunity and motivation for growth and positive change then we accept it as a challenge and try to acquire necessary knowledge and skills and learn how to transform it for growth and development.

Many of us believe that conflict arising from opposing ideas and opinions are to be encouraged. Controversies promote involvement in the group's work, quality and creativity in decision making, and commitment to implement the group's decisions.

To conclude although conflict is not always good, conflict is not always bad either. In fact conflict exists as a normal part of our everyday lives, and rather trying to make it go away, skills such as conflict analysis, communication, negotiation, and mediation can be learned to deal with the conflicts effectively.

In order to move a conflict habituated system to a peace system, we will need to change the way we think. The preamble of the Charter of the United Nations Educational, Social and Cultural Organization [UNESCO] echoes this sentiment, ***"since war begins in the minds of men, it is in the minds of men that the foundation of peace must be constructed."*** Change in the attitude and behavior can be achieved through formal or informal peace education.

It seems that there is now a growing awareness of the usefulness of peace education not only for children but also for adults. Formal or informal peace education can promote the development of an authentic consciousness that is necessary to change attitude and behavior in order to achieve the greater cooperation and peaceful problem solving. Peace education which involves learning new interpersonal skills and development of broader understanding of different cultures is therefore essential to enable us to strengthen the aspiration of peaceful coexistence and to enable us to function as global citizens and transform the present human conditions for the better.

As a matter of fact the focus of social peace building is also on addressing the underlying causes of conflict. This aspect of peace building in fact plays a vital and complementary role in the whole process of peace. In reality, it constructs a strong foundation for structural and political peace building processes to flourish, because it tries to involve a large number of people in the process.

The school-aged children in Afghanistan are in dire need for alternative education and career assistance to meet the demands of adulthood. Providing a learning and work environment where they feel challenged, respected and accountable as they strive to meet the demands of adulthood and engage in productive activities.

As a result of long years of war and conflict, poverty and cultural isolation have prevented the people of Afghanistan from becoming a prosperous and unified nation; and as sixty percent of its population is under 25, youth have been particularly affected. Many youth in Afghanistan still do not have access to education; the national literacy rate among youth is thirty-four percent for both boys and girls, and only eighteen percent for girls. In rural areas, where over seventy percent of youth reside, literacy among females is even lower at eight percent. Although girls have a legal right to attend school, fears of being stigmatized, harassed or worthless in marriage, deter them from attending schools.

One of the dangerous consequences of a lack of opportunity for young people is the potential development of detrimental behaviour. When such a large segment of the population lacks productive channels to direct their energies, a country runs the risk of widespread apathy, discontent, resentfulness, and disillusionment. Faced with few options for legitimate economic advancement, youth fall easy prey to criminal gangs, political groups, warlords, drug-lords, and fundamentalist associations.

According to the UNODC, the labour-intensiveness of drug production means that many young people work in family-owned poppy farms. Youth are also involved in the trafficking of narcotics, functioning as carriers to neighbouring countries, from where the drugs are then smuggled to the West. The narcotics trade also exposes Afghan youth to drug use and addiction.

The young generation of Afghanistan represents a cross-section of its society; and they are an integral, large and cross-cutting segment of wide range of Afghanistan's development ambitions, including good governance, peace, justice, security and economic development.

As in many other conflict situations, the young generation of Afghanistan has also been the victims of unbelievably horrific atrocities and injustices. The long term effects of conflict and militarization created a culture of violence that rendered children especially vulnerable after long years of war. The Afghan young generation has been the most affected ones, who have witnessed the catastrophes of war in its most disastrous manner. The culture of violence was nurtured in Afghanistan when the educational institutions by various regimes in Afghanistan were used as a tool to pursue their political agendas. Most of the educational institutions in Afghanistan suffered from politicization by various political factions and as a result the young generations acquired violent attitudes and behaviors even in the schools where the textbooks contained a lot of violent messages.

Due to ongoing war and conflict in Afghanistan, report of violence is the headlines of news broadcasted by the national and international media where children watch and listen to the news with full of violence. There is no or insufficient recreation facilities or activities to help develop positive attitude and creative thinking among the children. Unfortunately, the children of Afghanistan often experience violence where they live and where they go for education.

To address the challenges mentioned, it is essentially important to focus on initiatives to pursue a noble aim of promoting the culture of peace and non-violence amongst the new generation and divert the attention of children from the mentality of war and violence towards peaceful coexistence, co-operation and mutual respect.

All this can be achieved easily through integration of peace education in school curricula, teacher training on peace subjects and initiatives and meaningful activities where the young children of Afghanistan will have a unique opportunity to spend their free time for promotion of the knowledge, skills, attitudes and values needed to bring about positive behavioral changes.

In this way, it is possible to involve the children and youth in the process of peace and to make them responsible to take charge for a peaceful atmosphere in and after schools, to learn how to transform the daily life conflicts. They will also have the opportunity to know some of the many different ways for interacting, which will help them in the transformation process from mistrust to trust, from violent to non-violent behavior.

They will find a place where they can meet, exchange, practice of what they learn. The process of interaction will help them plan and organize events like peace- festivals, peace conference/concerts, star-walks, and more. Symbolic actions can also be encouraged where students can participate in planting trees, organizing exhibitions for peace [in paintings], writing essays and poems on peace.

All these will increase involvement of youths in meaningful activities and eventually contribute to personal development of children and youths for universally accepted values, attitude, skills and knowledge such as; creativity, decision making ability, leadership, civic participation, voluntarism, self-confidence and self-esteem, trust building, spirit of peaceful co-existence, effective communication and presentation skills, social support mechanism, self-motivated individuals and groups, global citizenship, positive interdependency relationship, interaction and networking with other similar groups and individuals within the country and around the world.

I strongly believe that integration of peace education and training of teacher in peace subject will:

- Enable children and youths to transform conflicts peacefully, and create conditions conducive to peace;
- Reduce violence of any nature [physical, cultural and structural];
- Reduce prejudices and stereotypes;
- Promote culture of peace and peaceful coexistence; and
- Develop new skills and attitude favorable not only to promote respect for diversity but also to pursue the initiatives to appreciate and celebrate diversity.

If we are to promote true peace and peaceful coexistence in our world, we have to come together to advocate very strongly at national and international levels to make peace education subject compulsory in schools and colleges.

*****

3

Education for Peace: A Need of the Hour

Lokanath Mishra

Abstract: Peace is the most urgent item on the agenda of humanity. No civilization is truly progressive without education and no education system is truly civilizing unless it is based on the universal principles of peace. However, peace is absent everywhere. Peace includes amity, friendship, harmony, concord, tranquility, repose, quiescence, truce, pacification, and neutrality. If we are to reach real peace in the world, we must begin with the children. The National Curriculum Framework NCF 2005 is planning to from a focus on implementing programmes in the schools to a centre for curricula development, training and research in peace education. Thus, education for peace relies on the strategy, which is more than class-room teaching learning about certain concepts and events related to peace and presented in textbooks. The broad objectives of non-violence education [NVE] include to promote non-violence values and attitudes [autonomy, responsibility, co-operation, creativity and solidarity]; to learn to live together, respecting the differences and similarities; to develop a co-operative learning based on dialogue and intercultural understanding; to adopt non-violence solutions to conflicts through mediations and conflict resolving strategies; to targeting the children and young people, particularly in the school educational process to integrate peace and non-violence in theory and practice; and to integrating non-violence in every aspect of teaching and learning processes, including curriculum development activities, teacher training and management of the educational institution.

Introduction

There is an increasing realization, especially during the last few decades, that the prevailing system of education in the world would not necessarily lead us towards a safe and peaceful future. It is important to note that the culture of violence and terrorism is generated and supported by the people preoccupied with their biases and hatred-based values; our education system is playing a complementary, if not causative, role in sustaining intolerance and extremism. In the cultural context it is said that today's so-called modernity and urbanity is leading us towards a society deprived of peace-generating social values. The values handed down from one generation to another through the modern structured education systems are based on curriculums approved by the interests of nation states.

Peace is the most urgent item on the agenda of humanity. No civilization is truly progressive without education and no education system is truly civilizing unless it is based on the universal principles of peace. However, peace is absent everywhere. In schools, families, and neighborhoods episodes of bullying, conflict, violence, and destructive behaviour are alarmingly high. In places of work, high levels of tension, rivalry, and mistrust exacts enormous personal and economic expense.

At the international level, monumental insecurities, inequities, conflicts, and violence based on political, racial, ethnic, and religious differences are bringing untold calamities to the masses of humanity—children, youth, and adults alike. In the final analysis, education is the most effective and universal tool for changing this unsettling state of affairs and for preparing every new generation of children and youth to learn the principles of peace and skills of peace building. The dawn of the new millennium, the United Nations has launched the decade for the *Culture of Peace*. The need for peace so acknowledged by an international body has brought it to the forefront of international forums and perhaps as one of the top priorities in our shared world agenda.

At The Hague Appeal for Peace conference in May 1999, most of the workshops, especially the youth workshops stressed the need for peace education while celebrating the unique potential of our youth. Youth is, by and large, free from intrinsically hatred-based preoccupations of the older generations. Youth, being an important beam of hope, should be targeted for bringing peace on the ground as well as in the minds of human beings living around the world. Peace is a word that is uttered almost as frequently as truth, beauty, and love. It may be just as elusive to define as these other virtues. Common synonyms for peace include amity, friendship, harmony, concord, tranquility, repose, quiescence, truce, pacification, and neutrality. Likewise, the peacemaker is the pacifier, mediator, intermediary, and intercessor. While some of these descriptions are appropriate, they are still quite limited in describing both the nature of peace and the role of the peacemaker. Any attempt to articulate the nature of peace and peacemaking, therefore, must address those conditions, which are favorable to their emergence. Freedom, human rights, and justice are among such prerequisites. Also included are proactive strategies such as conflict resolution, non-violent action, community building, and democratization of authority.

As Mahatma Gandhi has stated, ***"If we are to reach real peace in the world we must begin with the children."*** We must all become educators who will, in turn, learn the basic philosophical and pedagogical underpinnings of educating toward a more hopeful world. Peace education is defined as the pedagogical efforts to create a better world. The philosophy of peace education teaches love, non-violence, compassion and reverence for the environment and for all of life. The processes of peace education include empowering people with the skills of conflict resolution and with the knowledge to help create a more safe and sustainable world. Peace education involves care, compassion and concern-concern for oneself, for others and for the earth.

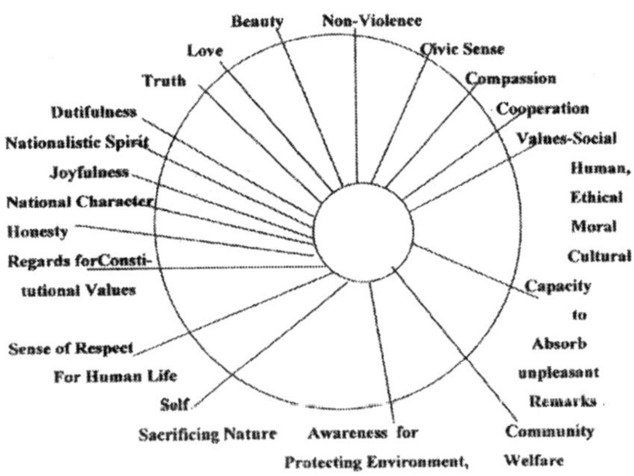

Factors which Contribute to Peaceful Environment and form part of Peace Education

Some revolutionary steps need to be taken for the practical implementation of peace education:

- The curriculum being taught in schools, especially at the primary level, must be geared towards making our kids responsible citizens with positive and peace loving thinking. The symbolic representation of words that is transferred to kids through elementary books needs to be changed from 'G for gun' to 'G for good';
- Schools structure must be based on equity and social justice, free from discrimination on the basis of class, caste or gender;
- Cultural activities are one of the most effective means of peace education. It channels the creative energy of youth from unhealthy activities to productive relationships;
- Respect for human rights is a very important dimension of peaceful human existence; and invariably peace is a human right. In this context, it is recommended that human rights education be introduced as a compulsory subject in secondary schools worldwide;
- In conflict prone regions [like Pakistan- India or the Balkans] youth exchange programs should be promoted and sustained through time in order to give students and youth exposure to pluralism, tolerance and respect for one another:
- Teachers should be given sufficient freedom to move out of the rut of curriculum. In most of the countries [esp. in the developing world] teachers are not enjoying their due rights and facilities;

- Special resources/ funds must be allocated to promote the concept of peace education; and
- However, we should not forget that peace education is not just something written in books, it's a concept- and awareness- a love to safeguard our world and future of our kids. It is not far off; it is just hidden in the dust of hatred and intolerance.

*****

4

Overcoming Communalization of Education-Path to Peace

Ram Puniyani

Abstract: Different fissiparous tendencies and diverse interests of social groups has been disturbing peace in the society. At global level the pursuit of control over raw materials has been one of the major causes of violence, prevalent all around. The sanction for this type of politics by global forces and the silent approval of the prejudices and biases underlying the violence are the major cause contributing to the process of divisiveness in the society. Again there are multiple mechanisms which strengthen the myths, biases and misconceptions about the targeted social groups. Gandhi and Nehru both had and inclusive vision of society, a vision steeped in the values of democracy. Their understanding of past was upholding the positive aspects of human culture and Indian society, due to which they could act as the binding glue for the Nation as a whole. This also got reflected in their politics and trainings which aimed at unity of Indian people and were also directed at global peace. The education, the percolation of divisive ideas through education and media has been on the rise during last three decades. The rootedness of people in the composite view of history has also been shaken due to the negativities of the social common sense percolated through divisive social organizations, education and media. All this is manifest in the present atmosphere, be it the prevalent culture or be it the concepts related to ***other*** the same thing is visible all around. How does one strive for peace in this scenario? How does one visualize peace and amity in this atmosphere? The propagation of values of amity, the look at history from the point of view of harmony on one side and integrative vision of Gandhi and Nehru have to form the core of the changes we envisage in the system of education and the pattern of media. This paper is an attempt to bring forth the problem of communal view of history and the glorification of wars. It demonstrates how the bypassing of the average people of society has been the central part history popularized so far. It is here that a social engagement with the past to build the peace in future has to pick up the threads of morality of culture; idealism of the values of freedom movement, with the place of Gandhi-Nehru at the center of the values, being put across. This paper is an attempt in that direction.

Introduction

India has witnessed regular recurrence of violence in the name of religion; the violence has seen the massive increase in intensity during last two decades. First in the decade of 1980s and then especially after post Babri demolition the massive pogroms were witnessed. The worst of this has been of course the one of Gujarat where on the pretext of Godhra train burning a systematic carnage was conducted with the assistance/collusion of the state machinery. After the anti-Sikh pogrom of 1984, the communalism manifested itself around Ram Temple, Rath yatras, demolition of Babri mosque and then the anti-Muslim pogrom, which gripped Mumbai. Gujarat carnage shook the nation to the core and has been a blot on Indian democracy. ***"Communalism is today the most serious threat facing the Indian people and the Indian nation. It can tear apart the Indian society and become a menace to the hard-won unity of Indian people and unleash forces of barbarism, as it did in Gujarat and earlier in Bombay, Bangalore, Jabalpur, Bhagalpur, Meerut, Moradabad, Punjab and Delhi."*** [Chandra, 2004, 5] Its nature has been changing over a period of years. ***"The inhuman cruelty committed during the course of communal riots, generally publicized by the media has demonstrated what communalism is capable of. But the character of communal cruelty has changed over years. Its manifestation is more intense and brutal."*** [Panikkar, 2008: V]

At global level terrorism has surfaced as a big set back to the peace process, this process all around has taken the garb of religion and thereby worsened the global scenario. Particularly after the attack of 9/11 2001, the term 'Islamic terrorism' has been popularized and propagated and the process of insane violence has stalked the World, more so in South Asia. The roots of this process while hidden in the lust for oil by the imperialist powers, has been presented as being related to Islam and its teachings, something totally false. The global media picked up words like Islamic terrorism and this did immense damage to the prevalent notions; worsening the peace scenario.

Communal Violence

Communal violence is the superficial manifestation of deeper communal politics. It targets the *other* community as the object of hate. Here the values of one's religion's humanism are contrasted with the practices of the *other* religions and the Hate is created for the other. It is on the basis of this hate that violence can go on in the streets. It is because of the doctored mass consciousness that this violence sustains itself. The doctoring of mass consciousness is also accompanied by Religion based group identity, which consolidates sections of society for this politics and the violence.

Communal violence is the festering wound on the body politic of Indian society. In pre-independence period the communal riots were a sort of reciprocal violence between Hindus and Muslims with the police [mainly British officers] intervening to restore peace. The nature of these riots after independence has changed in a significant way. First, the number of victims is more from Muslim community. Second, the loss of property is also more of Muslims and third, police plays a heavily partisan role in favor of the majoritarian communal forces. Initially it used be mainly the poor Muslims who were the major victims, but lately even the middle and upper class Muslims have also been drawn into this vortex.

Post-Independence Communal Violence

The post partition riots were followed by a period of comparative calm, in the decade of 50s, barring the one episode in eastern India and East Pakistan in 1950. This calm was broken in 60s when in 1962 and 1964 Jabalpur, Jamshelpur and Rourkela riots broke out. ***"Of the bloody pogroms in sixties, the ones at Ranchi, Bihar [1962] and Ahmedabad, Gujarat [1969] stand out as the major events. In seventies the Turkman Gate massacre of 1976 perpetrated by police, the riots in Moradabad [1980], Nellie, Naogaon, Assam [1983], Bhiwandi [1984] and Meerut [1987] have been the major ones in which more than a thousand lost their lives."*** [Khalidi, 1995: 19] There is a gradual change in the nature of riots in post-Independence India they ***"...have gradually acquired a character qualitatively different from those occurring during British period. These have no more remained assertions to gain economic and political space by subjugating different minority groups at local and or regional level. Instead they now draw their contents from a new form of political discourse that grew first in latent and subsequently in an explicit form through sustained introduction of a communal and divisive ideology."*** [Lobo and Das, 2006: 3]

Decade of Eighties

The Ramjanmabhoomi campaign left a big trail of blood in which more than thousand people lost their lives in 1989. The massacres of Bhagalpur, Hyderabad and Aligargh heralded the onset of bloody 80s, which has seen the peak of communal violence. Advani's rath yatra and post Babri demolition riots were one of the worst, the country has suffered so far. The post demolition riots gripped Mumbai, Surat, and Bhopal in a major way and many other places in a significant way. From

1960 to 1995 the incidences of riots have been on an upswing. A big proportion of these have been taking place in six states UP, Gujarat, Rajasthan, Bihar, Madhya Pradesh and Andhra. So far these riots' occurrence is mainly in cities, but involvement of villages is also there and has been in the rise but lately even the small towns and villages are also being drawn in the vortex.

Social Common Sense

Scholar-activist Asghar Ali Engineer points out, ***"Communal violence can never be explained in terms of religion alone. The religious factor is only apparent but not real. Religion is being exploited by vested interests to sit their own ends. Religion is emotionally appealing so acts as a powerful instrument of mobilization of potential and latent elements."*** [Engineer, 2004: 8] Why has the communal violence been growing, why has been the killing of innocent victims possible? And why does the large visible section of society quietly condone the killing of innocents? These questions have been dogging the minds of social activists. At various levels the issues raised by the communal politics have posed a serious challenge to the democratic values. One of the obstacles to the values of harmony comes from the notions held by the people about the minority community.

The Communal violence is rooted in the prevalent notions about minorities, which in turn create a hate other atmosphere and then any spark a plan by communal forces leads to violence, ***"Once society has been converted to a communal way of thinking by spreading communal ideology, the communalization of state institutions such as legislature, bureaucracy, police and educational institutions follow***

and so does communal violence characterized by riots and even genocide...no civilized society tolerates spreading of prejudices like that of racism [communalism is akin to racism] among school children, though in India it is still rampant." [Chandra, 2008: 9]

Prevalent Notions against Minorities

"The prevalent notions are encountered through the casual talk with the people, can be gleaned through the media, and are perceptible in different aspects of cultural expressions in the society. The ones' prevalent relate to the history, more so of medieval India, the so called Muslim period of Indian history, related to the ancient Indian history, related to the freedom movement and to the partition tragedy in particular." [Puniyani, 2006: 40] About the contemporary society there are many related to Muslims marrying more number of times, having twenty children, being aggressive as they eat meat, being conservative, being more unjust to 'their' women and also that all terrorists are Muslims. Many of these pertain to the Christian minorities also, like Christian missionaries are converting forcibly in the tribal areas. Also that Muslims should be sent to Pakistan and that Christians are foreigners. As the time passes most of these myths about minorities are becoming stronger by the day.

Perceptions Related to History

The root of history based myths is the communal historiography introduced by the British to pursue their aim of enslaving this country and also their policy of divide and rule. The mass consciousness has been doctored in a way that the minorities are looked at with suspicion. This doctoring of mass consciousness has been achieved by various mechanisms including the role of communal organizations boosting each other in all the ways. The intensity of these varies from place to place in India but its trajectory is the same. It is worst in Gujarat, followed by Jammu. In different parts of the country these prevail in one or the other form with varying shades of intensity.

It was James Mill who periodized Indian history on grounds of religion, the identities which had begun to become stronger during the British rule. The ancient India being Hindu Rashtra as it was the period of Hindu Kings got further boost from the theory propounded by Golwalkar that Aryans are the original inhabitants of this land. The Kings cannot be the markers of religion neither can the history be periodized as per the religion of Kings. At no point of time was the whole area ruled by the Kings belonging to one religion. Also that Kings kept invading different regions depending on their armed might. Kingdoms cannot be equated to modern nation states. The issue of Somnath temple and Ram Temple destruction are uppermost in the minds of the people. It is not realized that Kings destroyed temples for appropriating wealth and for showing their hegemony over the defeated kingdoms. ***"It is significant that generally temples are demolished in the territory of an enemy...it was symbol of the conquest by the sultan. Hindu rulers also did the same long before the Muslims had emerged as a political challenge to these Kingdoms."*** [Mukhia, 1994: 26]

Also British historiography was keen to present the Muslim rulers in the unfair light, as they had to win over the loyalty of subjects of the country. The left-over of divisive sectarian historiography exist in school texts in various forms. One example is very revealing. The medieval period is called as dark period of Indian History. A text book from Rajasthan prepared during BJP regime says, ***"The stagnation of Indian society during medieval period was fully taken advantage of by the Mughals. Since Mughal powers came to India to establish their rule they attempted to destroy the remaining religious unity...the aim of education became to educate Muslims and spread Islam, to attain physical luxuries and to attain political goals."*** [Apoorvanand, 2008: 14]

The BJP led NDA Government went on to brazenly communalize the text books. This worsened the problem. Even before that, ***"Indian History text books did contain distortions and evasions...The subtle demonization of Islam and Muslims, the evasive treatment of subject of partition, the lack of exposure or development of Dalits against injustice during the struggle for Independence....the scant treatment on the subject of the assassination of the father of nation, Gandhi are some of the most obvious examples."*** [Setalvad, 2002: 72]

Temple Destructions

The major misconceptions of history demonizing the present Muslim community are many. The major one pertains to the Babri Masjid as the British Gazetteer AS Beevraidge [Quoted in Panikkar, 1991: 34] put the unfounded question mark that there might have been a temple at the site where the mosque is located. There are infinite examples of the Hindu kings destroying Hindu Temples, Muslim Kings destroying mosques, like Aurangzeb destroying Golconda mosque when tribute was not paid by Tana Shah for few consecutive years. Hindu kings got the initial mosques made on the Malabar Coast. Tipu sultan went on to repair the temple Shrirangpatanam, which was destroyed by retreating Maratha armies. [Engineer, 1995]

The rule of kings was not meant for the sake of religion. Kings selected courtiers from all the religions. The nine Jewels of Akbar, The Muslim generals of Shivaji and Hakim Khan Sur assisting Rana Pratap in his battle against Akbar are too well known.

Communal ideology and politics began with the landlords and Princes, ***"Communalism enabled them to feel nationalistic without opposing imperialism, the foreign power which was then ruling and oppressing Indian people. It enabled them to combine personal safety with nationalist sentiments."*** [Chandra, 1994: 37] It was the British goal to have a foothold in South Asia due to which they were keen on partitioning the country and the Muslim and Hindu communal streams played in their hands.

The declining sections of elite, Landlords and Kings resorted to the politics in the name of Islam or Hinduism and that led to communal violence. ***"...by assigning the blame to 'other' communalism a sort of backdoor justification for one's own communalism is [or was] provided. Thus the Hindu, Muslim or Sikh communalists justified their own communalism by arguing that they were reacting to the communalism started by the other."*** [Chandra, 1988: 419] The communal view created a divisive social thinking leading to increasing violence over a period of time.

Gandhi in contrast had an all-inclusive view of nationalism, not based on religious identity. He points out in Hind Swaraj, ***"India cannot cease to be one nation because people belonging to different religions live in it. The introduction of foreigners does not necessarily destroy the nation, they merge in it. A country is one nation only when such a condition obtains in it. That country must have a faculty for assimilation; India has ever been such a country. In reality there are as many religions as there are individuals; but those who are conscious of the spirit of nationality do not interfere with one another's religion. If they do, they are not fit to be considered a nation. If the Hindus believe that India should be peopled only by Hindus, they are living in dreamland. The Hindus, the Mohammedans, the Parsis and the Christians who have made India their country are fellow countrymen, and they will have to live in unity, if only for their own interest. In no part of the world are one nationality and one religion synonymous terms; nor has it ever been so in India."*** [The Condition of India, Hindus and Mohammedans, Hind Swaraj http://www.mkgandhi.org/swarajya/coverpage.htm]

His identification and cultural adaptation of the ways of the mass of peasantry gave him the moral and practical leadership of the Indian National Movement in the days to come. Because of these methods, unlike the communalists, he was able to arouse and bring together millions under his leadership. His ideology and method brought in social peace. His patriotism was anti-British and was not confined to any single religious denomination. Gandhi had a deeply secular approach to the national freedom struggle, and continued to draw in its gambit people of all religions with equal enthusiasm.

Gandhi, Religion and Communalism

For Gandhi, religion mainly meant the ethical-moral component. He was concerned about focusing on and deriving from the core of social norms and values cutting across different religions. ***"I consider myself as good a Muslim as I am a Hindu and for that matter, I regard myself as equally good a Christian or a Parsi."*** [Gandhi and Communal Problems, CSSS, 1994: 6]. This quote of his has to be seen along with his two other more often cited quotes,***" For me, politics bereft of religion is absolute dirt, ever to be shunned"***, and ***"politics divorced from religion is like a corpse, fit only to be burnt."***

To get the full meaning of his *religiosity*, one has to understand that his religiosity transcends the boundaries of prevalent 'religious institutions'. His religion includes the whole humanity in its sweep and does not see enemies in different religious traditions. Essentially in the tradition of Bhati and Sufi saints he identified religion with moral values and not identity. It was because of this that communal amity was the core of his work.

Despite the best efforts of Gandhi, the combination of British policy of divide and rule, and the politics unleashed by communalists resulted in the partition of the country. The violence, the marker of communal ideology did persist, and kept resurfacing in more dangerous form from the decade of 1980. It was not religion due to which the clashes, violence and later the partition tragedy took place; it was the political interests of the declining sections of society which were couched as religious interests.

Despite the contributions of Gandhi-Nehru the many narratives of freedom movement, coming through text books are divisive. This hangover of British communal historiography persists with freedom movement narratives as well; the same applies to the versions prevalent in Pakistan. In Pakistan the things are turned the other way around from what they are in India. ***"The history of freedom movement taught to school children in India and Pakistan is framed by a deep awareness of the 'other'. In both cases, the scene of what happened in the past is intertwined with the current evolving perception of the 'other'. This applies to older history as well..."*** [Krishna Kumar, Prejudice and Pride, Viking, New Delhi, 2001: 29]

Role of Education

The school books prevalent in the state level boards were/are having such inherent biases. These were a sort of leftover of the British legacy. This communal view of History was/is being actively promoted by communal streams. This also formed a major chunk of underlying viewpoint which was the base of school history books in the states. This view introduced prejudice, while the National Council for Education Research and Training [NCERT] books brought out during 1980s, were good and rational. These NCERT books were replaced during the BJP led NDA regime. All in all the school books, RSS propaganda through word of mouth and its affiliates and mechanisms developed by it, through media has already prepared a fertile ground for the communalization of the social space, more so the middle classes.

With the violence spreading to villages and with the RSS affiliates like Vishwa Hindu Parishad reaching the villages the communalization also began to reach the villages. RSS has systematized the spread of hate through tens of thousands of its Sarswati Shishu Mandirs and Vidya Bharati primary and secondary schools, and through its shakhas. ***"Part of the Hate project is to portray all communities other than Hindus as foreigners in India, who are disloyal and trust, particularly the Muslims, who the RSS founder K. B. Hedgewar described as hissing yavan snakes."*** [Mukherjee et all: 18] Communalism has been built up in India and one can gauze the danger of this phenomenon from the fact that, ***"Gandhiji, the fiercest defender of and fighter for civil liberties, made one exception. He believed that state power should be used to ban 'all literature circulated to promote communalism, fanaticism and hatred..."*** [Mukherjee: 19]

Violence, Minorities and Inquiry Commissions

While the violence has multiple social reasons, in popular perceptions the minorities are supposed to be the cause for the same. Here victim is presented as the culprit. As far as communal violence goes a new myth has been making rounds that Muslims start the communal violence as they are violence in nature. This is the highest success of the Right wing organizations. The minority is generally cornered and then attacked mostly in a preplanned manner, but it is projected as if minorities, Muslims start the riots. Most of the investigation commissions have pointed that that the riots are engineered by a group affiliated to RSS and many a riots are well planned by communal organizations right in advance like the one of Gujarat. ***"By now it has been propagated successfully that Muslims start the riots and then Hindus retaliate. Teesta Setalvad*** [Who Casts the First Stone, Communalism Combat, March 98] ***by citing the extracts from five commissions of inquiry shows that truth is other way around. It is interesting that while the inquiry commissions have one type of conclusion the popular notions are totally against that and are getting deeply ingrained in people's minds."***

Post 9/11: Islam, Muslims and Violence

In the aftermath of various acts of terror, a prevalent formulation that all Muslims are not terrorists but all terrorists are Muslims is doing rounds and has become part of social common sense, but it has nothing to do with truth. Terrorism is a political process resorted to by a section of people whose democratic rights are strangulated, who perceive that the injustice which has been perpetrated on them will not get justice in the times to come and that revenge is the only option in such a situations. It is a political process and religion or a religious community has nothing to do with it. Neither any religion teaches to kill the innocents [that is what the terrorists do] nor are the terrorists the people chosen by that religious community to undertake such ghastly acts on their behalf.

The definition of terror is also not well formulated, the person appearing as terrorist, for some he may sound as freedom fighter for another set of people. The examples of Bhagat Singh, the Kashmiri militants and LTTE are few such. We have seen the ghastly terrorist acts by Khailstanis, the ULFA, the likes of Timothy McVeigh; who dropped a bomb on Oklahoma out of frustration, we also know of a Jewish bomber dropping a bomb on a Hotel in Cairo in 1942 and Buddhist monks indulging in such violent acts in Sri Lanka and Thailand. The backdrop of these countries will tell us the political nature of the acts and that these are not meant to serve any religion.

The trajectory of terrorism in which some Muslims have participated has roots in the oil politics at global level, in the Kashmir problem and in the rising communal problem in Indian context. The formation of Al Qaeda by the United States to drive away the Russian armies from Afghanistan is too well known by now. The Kissinger doctrine, *Asians should fight Asian* was employed to train Al Qaeda by CIA to fight the Soviet occupation of Afghanistan. Special Madarasas were set up, which indoctrinated a section of Muslim youth in to Jihad. The meaning given to this word was that jihad is killing of non-believers, communists in this case, an innovation which worked wonder for the US policy. The Muslim youth were dangled the carrot of 72 virgins in Jannat once they lay down their life in pursuance of the US goal of capturing Afghanistan after evicting the Soviet armies.

The demonization of Islam and Muslims began with the US propaganda in the wake of Ayatollah's revolution in Iran and it was systematically built up with every US intervention in the West Asia, attack on Iraq, the occupation of Afghanistan the occupation of Iraq and also after the Al Qaeda attack on WTC. The demonization of Islam and Muslims has been a very systematic process akin to demonization of communists in the cold war era, McCarthyism and the accompanying propaganda.

Noam Chomsky explains this doctrine as *manufacturing consent* for the goals of US foreign policy, which are achieved by US administration through various mechanisms, media being the central key to this doctoring of mass consciousness. This and other means employed by the US administration to demonize Muslims has been outlined very well by Mahmood Mamdani's *Good Muslim Bad Muslim* [Permanent Black, Delhi, 200] and by Tariq Ali in *Clash of Fundamentalisms* [Rupa, Dehli, 2002] and *Bush in Babylon* [Leftword, 2003], where both these researchers have given the details of the US policymakers documents and the mechanism to demonize the targeted country and the people.

The other Minority: Christians

The schools books, other presentations of History and religion have been deeply influenced by Not to be left behind, the Christian minorities have also been 'taken care of', more so since 1996. It was the time when RSS affiliate Vanvasi Kalyan Ashrams work came to fruition and with this the Christian missionaries were tagged with the image that their primary work is conversions. Amongst various reasons for taking up Christians for attacking one was also partly related to Sonia Gandhi, a Catholic coming to the fore in the political space. Her unexpected mass appeal bowled the opponents over. She was called as *foreigner* and a sinister campaign was initiated which was picked up by section of Congress itself to break their own party. Today apart from the conversion bogey the threat of a foreigner ruling the country and India coming under the grip of Italian rule is being conjured up in a serious way to section of middle classes. The language press in particular has fanned the myths about minorities in a serious way. The fear amongst the Christians living in the villages is going up. ***"Missionaries have been stripped naked and paraded through the streets, even burnt alive, nuns have been gang raped, churches have been razed to the ground and Bible and other literature has been burnt...The heightened animosity and violence against Christians coincides with the of BJP at the center."*** [Panikkar, 1999]

While in cities the parents of all shades of political thinking vie to put their children in the Christian missionary schools, in the small remote places, the Christians are projected a foreigners. The major strategy is to work for manufacturing these myths, stereotypes and keep percolating them on constant basis apart from keeping producing new ones on continuous basis. The social space today seems to be largely gripped by the ideas produced in the RSS Shakhas and its head office, and it has serious repercussions on the political chessboard of the country.

Religion: Social Interaction and Peace

The presentation of history in text books and popular accounts is heavily influenced by the British introduced communal historiography. Even the religious traditions were presented in a distorted manner or in a selective way. The interactive traditions which untied the people were by passed, ignored. As such Sufi, Bhakti traditions in medieval times Gandhi during freedom movement united the people along the moral values of religion. The education and social thinking does not much take this into account.

Sufis attracted a large following among the lower classes and castes. It was their unorthodox and simple lifestyle, which attracted large number of low castes to convert to Islam. ***"They were much closer to the masses; both Hindus as well as Muslims.Their majars [holy places] were open to all irrespective of their religious following. Sufis were basically upholding the spiritual side of Islam, and it can be said that it was a revolt against the rigidities of Islam, propagated mainly by the Ulema. One of the great Sufi saints Muhiuddin Ibn Arabi founded the doctrine of Wahahdat-al-wujud i.e. Unity of being, which promoted spiritual universalism, in turn demolishing the barriers of caste and creed. These doctrine states that the real being is one and we are all its manifestations, this brought in harmony amongst followers of different religions."*** [Engineer: 26]

It is interesting to note that the Sufi saint's writings were very close to the people. Baba Farid wrote poetry in Punjabi and his writings are a part of Granth Sahib, the holy book of the Sikhs. Baba Farid's most distinguished follower was Nizamuddin Auliya, who proudly used to say that there were as many ways of worshipping God as there are particles of sand. He was very fond of listening to bhajans, being touched equally by bhajans and quawallis. His respect for local traditions was tremendous.

The interaction of the practices of these two religions has been very well summarized by well-known scholar B. N. Pandey, ***"Islam and Hinduism which appeared at the start so anti-thetical, at last intermingled, each one stirred the***

profoundest depth of the other and from their synthesis grew the religion of Bhakti and Tasawwaf, the religion of love and devotion, which swept the hearts of millions following different religions and sects in India. The current of Islamic Sufism and Hindu Bhakti combined into a mighty stream which fertilized old desolate tracts and changed the face of the country. It was this spirit of India which achieved apparently an impossible task of reconciling the puritanical severity and awe inspiring transcendence of Islam into luxuriant fullness and abundance of form and the intuitive perception of their immanent unity with Hinduism, and created those monuments of art, literature, painting, music, poetry and love inspired religion which are the heritage of Indian History, during the middle ages." [Quoted in Engineer: 14]

Gandhi had his own unique interpretation of religion, an interpretation which was very close to the psyche of Indian people, ***"I consider myself as good a Muslim as I am a Hindu and for that matter, I regard myself as equally good a Christian or a Parsi."*** [Harijan, May 25, 1937: 16] This quote of his has to be seen along with his two other more often cited quotes, ***"For me, politics bereft of religion is absolute dirt, ever to be shunned", and "politics divorced from religion is like a corpse, fit only to be burnt."*** This is an understanding in which the very concept of *we* and *they* gets abolished. Gandhi's nationalism represented the emerging nation. Though expressed in religious language, it was not bound to any single religion. For him, India was to be a secular state where all religions will be respected equally at social level but none of them will be the claimant to guide the state. While at the political level, morality has to rein supreme, ***"In India, for whose fashioning I have worked all my life, every man enjoys equality of status, whatever his religion is. The state is bound to be wholly secular."*** [Harijan, August 31, 1947], and, ***"religion is not the test of nationality but is a personal matter between man and God",*** [Ibid: 90], and, ***"religion is a personal affair of each individual, it must not be mixed up with politics or national affairs."*** [Ibid: 90]

Religion: Peace Education

The impact of communally tainted education has communalized social thinking, social common sense, creating emotional wall amongst different communities; it is also resulting in the retardation of social development. The kernel of present efforts for peace lies in the process of building bridges amongst communities and that process can be started only by a genuine dialogue amongst people of different faiths, by coming close to each other by abolishing the artificial boundaries created by the politics of hate being practiced by various forces, globally and locally. These dialogues amongst different religious communities are needed at all the levels, starting from localities to the leadership of religions, scholars of religions, the activists engaged in dispelling hate from the society, and those working for human rights, all of them need to be involved in this process of dialogue.

We need to look into the recent high level committee of UN which went on to counter the thesis of clash of civilizations put forward by the US professor Samuel Huntington. This thesis forms the cover for the US ambitions for its aggressions in the West Asia. The UN committee (http://www.unaoc.org/repository/report.htm) has put forward that there is no clash between civilizations, as a matter of fact civilization have an alliance for a better tomorrow. On the similar lines one will like to say that there is no clash between the moral values of religions, it is the alliance between these values that the human race can look forward to a better future, a future which will eliminate poverty, hunger, disease and misery from the world. It is this alliance which will ensure that the focus of world policies has to be brought back to the issue of Human rights of weaker sections of society.

There can be no peace without justice. The education for peace involves the efforts to look at the real goals of the political forces, which are abusing the name of religion for their political goals. It's imperative that moral values of religions are highlighted and in the education for peace the moral/value aspects of religion must be given the foremost place. With these misconceptions and the mix up between religion and politics it is difficult to talk of peace.

The UN Resolution 52/13, says, ***"A culture of peace is based on respect for human rights, democracy and tolerance, the promotion of development, education for peace, the free flow of information and the wider participation of women as an integral approach to preventing violence and conflicts, and efforts aimed creation of conditions for Peace and its consolidation."*** The focus on global democratic values and participation of all is the crux for peace education, more so at a time when the UN itself has been bypassed by the mighty nation of the World.

In contemporary context peace education has to address the global political hegemony of powerful nations and the moral values of religion and the fact that these are two separate things. ***"In general, peace education can be understood from a negative or a positive perspective. Negatively peace education is learning how to react to situations of conflict or war, or how to avoid them. Positively peace education is a long term pro-active strategy. It aims to promote peaceful who are equipped with appropriate knowledge, skills and attitudes to encounter the many conflicts life offers."*** [Gonsalves, 2003: VII] Thus the responsibility and understanding of peace workers has to range from situations creating conflict-war to the human rights and values of global democracy. ***"Traditionally peace education is understood in three ways: empowering people through peace keeping, peacemaking and peace building. Peace keeping means learning conflict preventing skills or ways to deter violence Peacemaking helps opposite parties*** [persons, groups, nations] ***resolve conflict. Peacemaking means motivating people to choose peaceful solutions to problems and encouraging them to live peaceful lives."*** [Gonsalves: VIII]. ***"Unlike peacemaking and peace keeping, which are related to warfare and settlement of conflicts, the concept of peace building [is] the constitution of the new environment-the transformation of deficient national structures and capabilities and–the strengthening of new democratic institutions?"*** [Ghali, 1992]

Today unlike never before the human race is confronted with splits in the name of religion as politics is adorning the clothes of religion. The multi-pronged approach for peace has to have peace education as the kernel of efforts of mankind.

Bibliography:

- Ali, Tariq. 2002. *Clash of Fundamentalisms*. Delhi [India]: Rupa.
- Ali, Tariq. 2003. *British in Babylon* in Leftword.
- Apoorvanand. 2008. *Rajasthani Skooli Pustakon Men Jansnahad*, page 14. Delhi [India]: ANHAD.
- Beveridge, AS. 1991. *Baburnama*, pp. LXXVII in Panikkar, in S Gopal's *Anatomy of Confrontation*. Delhi [India]: Penguin.
- Chandra, Bipan. 2004. *Communalism*. New Delhi [India]: Anamika Publishers.
- Chandra Bipan. 2008. Foreword to Aditya Mukherjee, Mridula Mukherjee and Sucheta Mahajan's *RSS School Texts and Murder of Mahatma Gandhi*. Delhi [India]: Sage.
- Chandra, Bipan. 1994. *Historian of Modern India and Communalism* [Selected Writings on Communalism] Delhi [India]: Peoples Publishing House.
- Chandra, Bipan, 1988. *India's Struggle for Freedom*. Delhi [India]: Penguin.
- Engineer, Asghar Ali. 2004. *Communal Riots After Independence*. Mumbai [India]: CSSS and Delhi [India]: Shipra
- Gandhi, MK. *The Condition of India, Hindus and Mohammedans in Hind Swaraj* http://www.mkgandhi.org/swarajya/coverpage.htm
- Engineer, Asghar Ali. *Medieval History and Communalism,* page 26. Mumbai [India]: Center for Syudy of Society and Secularism.
- Gandhi, MK [ed.]. 1947, May 25. Harijan.
- Ghali, Boutros Boutros. 1992. *An Agenda for Peace, UN Secretary General*, quoted in Gonsalvees Peter Peace Education Volume- I. 2003. Mumbai [India]: Don Bosco Communications.

- Khalidi, Omar. 1995. *Indian Muslims Since Independence*. New Delhi [India] Vikas Publishing House.
- Kumar, Krishna. 2001. *Prejudice and Pride*. New Delhi [India]: Viking.
- Lobo, Lancy and Das, Biswaroop. 2006. *Communal Violence and Minorities*, Jaipur [India]: Rawat Publications.
- Mukhia, Harbans. 1994. *Medieval History and the Communal Approach* [Selected Writings on Communalism]. Delhi [India]: Peoples Publishing House.
- Mamdani Mahmood. 2002. *Good Muslim Bad Muslim*. Delhi [India]: Permanent Black.
- Panikkar, KN. 1999, January 30. *Towards a Hindu Nation*. New Delhi [India]: Frontline.
- Panikkar, KN. 2008. *Rise of Fascism*. New Delhi [India]: Human Rights Law Network.
- Puniyani, Ram. 2006. *Breaking Silence*. Delhi [India]: Anhad.
- Setalvad, Teesta. 1998, March. *Who Casts the First Stone*. Mumbai [India]: Communalism Combat (http://www.unaoc.org/repository/report.htm).
- Setalvad, Teesta. 2002. *Indian Textbooks: A Means of Controlling the Mind* in Abhay Kumar and Samik Lahiri's [ed] *Behind the Blackboard*. Delhi [India]: SFI Publications.

*****

Part 2
Gandhian Perspectives

1
Education and Peace: A Gandhian Perspective

Ravindra Kumar

Abstract: It is needless to mention about the role and importance of education in the life of man. Education is the only means for the all-round development of humans. The pathway to human prosperity and peace follows the lanes of education with the condition that its direction should be right and founded on values. Great men, reformers, thinkers and philosophers have from time-to-time guided humanity in the right path. Many of them have given exemplary suggestions to make education a prime focus and significance of them cannot be diminished even today. This chain of thought emphasizes Mahatma Gandhi's desire for the complete physical and mental development of man through value education for his self-reliance, which paves the way for his prosperity and peace.

Introduction

"By education I mean an all-round drawing out of the best in child and man-body, mind and spirit. Literacy is not the end of education or even the beginning."

–MK Gandhi [Harijan: July 31, 1937]

Education certainly is a means to all-round progress of man. In other words, the pathway to human-development goes through the lanes of education. Moreover, true education is the sole basis of achieving one's purpose in life. It is education, which can ascertain ultimate peace for a human being.

Needless to say, the importance of education in man's life cannot be described in words. In addition, the essence of all the ancient scriptures, messages of scholars and thinkers of repute have always categorically expounded the significance of education in human life. By illustrating the mutual relationship between the education and peace, they have also declared education as the means and basis of peace. Furthermore, they enlighten people of the importance of education in all walks of life, in particular, its role in making life prosperous and peaceful under the prevailing circumstances. Further, the implications in the absence of true education, especially in creating an atmosphere of disharmony and conflict are examined. In this regard the following *Shloka* from an oldest Hindu scripture is worth quoting here:

"माता शत्रु पिता वैरी येन बालो न पाठितः
न शोभते सभा मध्ये हंस मध्ये वाको यथा।"

"Mata Shatru Pita Vairi Yen Balo Na Pathitah, Na Shobhate Sabha Madhye Hans Madhye Vako Yatha"

Meaning thereby: The parent who does not facilitate and guide the child for studies is like the greatest enemy of the child. The presence of an uneducated person in the company of educated people is like a goose in the company of swans.

The utility, significance and importance of education are inevitable at all levels in all walks of life. It develops into the most beautiful and valuable ornament of human life.

Now, before further discussion regarding mutual relations between education and peace, we should understand the meaning and purpose of the both-education and peace-separately. To do so with particularly emphasis on the Gandhian view is important and considered the prudent approach for this article.

Education

The English meaning for education is derived from the Latin word *Educare*, which further relates to *Educere*, the symbolic of manifestation or expression. This definition reveals the inner capability of man that guides him continuously at various levels. The whole process, which leaves an impact upon the mind, character and physical strength, plays a vital role in human development. It accords continuity to intellect, knowledge and values, which provides the base and scope of education.

If we analyze education from the Indian viewpoint, education [*Shiksha*] is one of the six *Vedangas*.[1] Clarity of understanding and systematic method or the orders, which are the basics for the all-round development of one's personality, are within its domain. Hence, the educational process is fully dedicated to continuity; it is for growth or for accumulation; it is the means to lead a human being on the pathway to prosperity in prevailing circumstances on the basis of knowledge and accomplishments.

Peace

The use of popular English word *peace* can be found in words like *Pax* [Vulgate], *Eirene* [Greek] and *Shalom* [Hebrew]. Besides desiring harmony in day-to-day human practices at individual and social levels, the urge for a situation free from conflicts and struggles is derived here. Generally, a situation free from tension, struggle, dispute or conflict, particularly in socio-economic spheres, is considered the state of peace in this context. This phenomenon signifies the absence of fight or war between or among the nations and is generally the accepted notion of peace at the international level. It is almost the same in the Indian perspective. Popular Hindi words, which are derived from *Samskrit*, such as *Vishram*, *Nivriti*, *Nistabdha* and *Ananda* are used to describe a state of peace.

Despite this similarity between the Western and Indian perspectives, peace is not a motionless state even according to ancient philosophical thought. Peace is not a situation of the status quo. The state of peace provides man the pathway to progress in a tension-free atmosphere. Within a state of peace, efforts are made for healthy co-existence to extend the welfare of the people. Therefore, the state of peace is in fact dynamic. It fills people with enthusiasm and inspires them to move forward.

Education and Peace

Evidently education is the basis for the all-round development of man; it is the means of developing his personality. Moreover, it is the process that helps make one's life purposeful. All constructive and welfaristic conditions that may be required for the purpose are also inherent in this process. Similarly, peace, despite a state free from dispute, conflict and war, is also an active and dynamic state in which there is a call to go forward. New benefits are expected in a state of peace. It is the pathway to progress without any fear and confusion. Therefore, one can say that education and peace are linked to one-another. They supplement each other as both contribute to the development and welfare of each and every human being on this planet.

Gandhian View

According to Mahatma Gandhi, education is an unending exercise [filled with devotion-*Sadhana*][2] till death. For him, only education can act as a means to a successful life. Likewise, ***"education can help mould and shape the human body, mind and character in such a manner that they may act as the means to achieve joy and efficiency."***[3]

Categorically, education as expounded through Gandhi's imagination and explanation is a means to guide and lead a human-being from his birth to death. It helps man achieve his goal. The goal however, according to many philosophies including the *Vedic*-Hindu, could be the attainment of the *Mukti* or *Moksha*, or *Nirvana* [liberation] that it is considered as the highest stage of peace.

Furthermore, the imagination and explanation of Mahatma Gandhi about education could be better comprehended by the following statement of Kishorelal Mashruwala[4]:

"[This] ***works for the all-round growth of man right from the beginning till the end. Its ultimate aim is to turn human knowledge into his ability. It is for the purpose of making his life worthy and meaningful, and it is not only for earning his livelihood."***[5]

Mahatma Gandhi wrote many articles on education from time-to-time. On several occasions, besides addressing students and teachers, he issued worthy statements regarding its meaning, purpose and importance in life. We can draw the following viewpoint particularly for the purpose of this short article:

1. The prime aim of education is to make a man self-dependent;
2. The purpose of education is to make the one efficient and skilful; and
3. The objective of education is to guide and lead him to the pathway to progress in the prevailing situation of space and as per the demand of time so that he could ascertain his physical and mental development to achieve a goal in life for himself on the one hand and he could equally contribute to the society, nation and the globe on the other.

After analyzing the above three points, it can be said with certainty that the Gandhian concept of education is one of the most important views on the subject for us today. This concept urges for man to be self-dependent, skilful and efficient. Thereby, his goal and objective, to achieve true education will be open. Not only this, the Gandhian view of education can play the vital role in the establishment of peace not only at the national level but also at the international level.

References:

1. The six *Vedangas*are in fact the six auxiliary disciplines traditionally associated with the study and understanding of the *Vedas* [four in number]. They are *Shiksha*, *Kalpa* [ritual], *Vyakarna* [grammar], *Nirukta* [etymology], *Chandas* [meter] and *Jyotisha* [astronomy].

2. For, he used the words *'Akhand Sadhana'*. Particularly, the word *Sadhana* has a broad and deep meaning; besides being important in human life, it is a well-known concept in Indian philosophy.

Saadhana: [साधना], in fact, is also the way or a means of accomplishing something through spiritual practice, which includes not only a variety of disciplines of the *Vedic*-Hindu tradition, but also the Jain, Buddhist and Sikh traditions followed in order to achieve certain spiritual objectives, or ultimately the *Moksha* or *Nirvana* [salvation], the goal of human life.

3. Kumar, Ravindra. 1999. *Essays on Gandhism and Peace*, page 10. Meerut [India]: Krishna Publication.

4. Kishorlal Mashruwala [1890-1952], a freedom fighter, Gandhian scholar and thinker was the editor of Harijan weekly started by the Mahatma.

5. Kumar, Ravindra. 1999. *Essays on Gandhism and Peace*, page 10. Meerut [India]: Krishna Publication.

*****

2

In Quest of Alternative Civilization: The Gandhian Education Revisited

Rachana Chakraborty

Abstract: Gandhi elaborated his thoughts on education in his seminal article on education published in the Harijan on July 31, 1937. He wrote, ***"By education I mean an all-round drawing out of the best in child and man - body, mind and spirit."*** Gandhi probably felt that the intervention of the colonial state had created a form of education that was totally out of touch with the roots of Indian reality. It could not touch the lives of the millions and tended to convey a borrowed identity on minuscule elite. He therefore, was primarily concerned with the need to formulate an alternate, meaningful, non-violent, non-exploiting, self -sufficient education system that would be truly reflective of the village –based, multi-cultural Indian society. As the spearhead of a silent social revolution, it would confer a new identity to the future self-confident post-colonial society.

Introduction

While delivering a talk at the University of Berkeley, the

visiting professor, Ekanath Easwaran reflected, ***"Historians of the future, I believe, will look upon this century not as the atomic age but as the age of Gandhi..."***[1] The audience appreciated the speaker's sentiment though not fully comprehending it. It is interesting to note that Gandhi's importance in history or in Indian life was not limited to his leadership in the country's struggle for freedom alone. He was interested in the making of an alternative civilisation.[2] As education has a very definite role to play in the ordering of society, and imparts a particular identity to the society it represents, a reviewing of Gandhian thoughts on education as the catalyst of socio-economic change becomes imperative.

Gandhi elaborated his thoughts on education, in his seminal article on education published in the Harijan of 31 July, 1937. He wrote, ***"By education I mean an all-round drawing out of the best in child and man-body, mind and spirit. Literacy is not the end of education nor even the beginning. It is only one of the means whereby man and woman can be educated. Literacy in itself is no education. I would therefore begin the child's education by teaching it a useful handicraft and enabling it to produce from the moment it begins its training. I hold that the highest development of the mind and the soul is possible under such a system of education. Only every handicraft has to be taught not merely mechanically as is done today but scientifically, i.e., the child should know the why and the wherefore of every process. I am not writing this without some confidence, because it has the backing of experience. This method is being adopted more or less completely***

wherever spinning is being taught to workers. I have myself taught sandal-making and even spinning on these lines with good results. This method does not exclude knowledge of history and geography. But I find that this is best taught by transmitting such general information by word of mouth. One imparts ten times as much in this manner as by reading and writing. The signs of the alphabet may be taught later when the pupil has learnt to distinguish wheat from chaff and when he has somewhat developed his or her tastes. This is a revolutionary proposal, but it saves immense labour and enables a student to acquire in one year what he may take much longer to learn. This means all round economy. Of course, the pupil learns mathematics whilst he is learning his handicraft. Given the right kind of teachers, our children will be taught the dignity of labour and learn to regard it as an integral part and means of their intellectual growth, and to realize that it is patriotic to pay for their training through their labour. The core of my suggestion is that handicrafts are to be taught, not merely for productive work, but for developing the intellect of the pupils. You have to train the boys in one occupation or another. Around this special occupation you will train up his mind, his body, his handwriting, his artistic sense, and so on. He will be a master of the craft he learns..."[3]

After his return from South Africa, Gandhi travelled across India and saw poverty and idle hands face to face. It generated his talisman, ***"recall the face of the poorest and the weakest man/woman whom you have seen and ask yourself the***

step you contemplate is going to be of any use to him / her."

With this vision he began to search for a solution to banish hunger, poverty, unemployment and inequality.[4] Gandhi probably felt that the intervention of the colonial state had created a form of education that was totally out of touch with the roots of Indian reality. It could not touch the lives of the millions and tended to convey a borrowed identity on minuscule elite. He therefore, was primarily concerned with the need to formulate an alternate, meaningful, non-violent, non-exploiting, self -sufficient education system that would be truly reflective of the village –based, multi-cultural Indian society. As the spearhead of a silent social revolution[5], it would confer a new identity to the future self-confident post-colonial society.

Krishna Kumar, Professor of Education at Delhi University, wrote that ***"no one rejected colonial education as sharply and as completely as Gandhi did, nor did anyone else put forward an alternative as radical as the one he proposed."*** Gandhi's critique of Western, particularly English, education was part of his critique of Western civilization as a whole.[6]

Professor Kumar argued that with the gradual strengthening of colonial hold over India, and the concomitant advance of English education, the school curriculum gradually became dissociated from the Indian child's everyday reality and cultural environment, representing as it did, the alien values and ideals of officialdom.[7] In Gandhi's perception, colonial education was an instrument with which the state maintained its power. The medium of instruction being a foreign language created a barrier between the millions in the villages and the few thousands of the upper crust. Moreover, the colonial system emphasized learning by rote without questioning its efficacy in Indian society. Gandhi's basic education plan implied the end of the teacher's subservience to the prescribed textbook and curriculum. It presented a concept of learning that could not be fully implemented with the help of textbooks. More important was the freedom and authority that the basic education plan gave the teacher in matters concerning the school curriculum. It was a libertarian plan, similar to Tolstoy's and Tagore's in as much as it denied the state the power to decide what precisely the teacher must do in the classroom.[8]

In 1921, Gandhi wrote to Rabindranath Tagore, ***"I want the cultures of all the lands to be blown about my house as freely as possible. But I refuse to be blown off my feet by any. I refuse to live in other people's houses as an interloper, a beggar or a slave....I refuse to put the necessary strain of learning English upon my sisters for the sake of false pride or questionable social advantages. I would have young men and women with literary tastes to learn as much English and other world languages as they like, and then expect them to give the benefit of their learning to India and the world, like a Bose, a Roy or the Poet himself. But I would not have a single Indian to forget, neglect or be ashamed of his mother tongue, or to feel that he or she cannot think or express the best thoughts in his or her own vernacular."***[9]

Jawaharlal Nehru depicted the contrast between the two great men somewhat differently. He said, ***"No two persons could be so different from one-another in their make up***

or temperaments. Tagore, the aristocratic artist, turned democrat with proletarian sympathies, represented essentially the cultural tradition of India, the tradition of accepting life in the fullness thereof and going through it with song and dance. Gandhi, more a man of the people, almost the embodiment of the Indian peasant, represented the other ancient tradition of India, that of renunciation and asceticism. And yet Tagore was primarily the man of thought, Gandhi of concentrated and ceaseless activity. Both, in their different ways had a world outlook, and both were at the same time wholly Indian. They seemed to present different but harmonious aspects of India and to complement one another."[10]

Compared to Tagore, Gandhi's rejection had a sharper edge to it because his critique of colonial education was a part of his overall critique of Western Civilization. The fact that Western men had spent ***"all their energy, industry and enterprise in plundering and destroying other races"*** was evidence enough for Gandhi that Western Civilization was in a state of *sorry mess.*[11] In Gandhi's perception all the evils of the 20th century-colonial exploitation, poverty, war, disease- were the results of industrialization which in its turn precipitated competition, consumerism, atomized society that ultimately destroyed human values. Gandhi was fundamentally opposed to the entire edifice of bourgeoisie society – as argued by Partha Chatterjee.[12] In his Hind Swaraj he launched an attack on every aspect of Western civilization in order to prove how evil and how harmful it was. He mercilessly criticized the machine –based industrial civilization of Europe, trapped in a vicious circle of greed and violence, and therefore, devoid of moral force. Such a society could never be the ideal for India to emulate.[13] Thus true education, according to Gandhi was one that brought about a harmonious development of all the aspects of the human personality. It would also draw out and stimulate the spiritual, intellectual and physical faculties.[14] There is no doubt, that Gandhi accorded character –building a central place in his plan of primary education, based on the promotion of the practice of ahimsa and the pursuit of truth. He believed that education could come through a proper exercise and training of both mind and body and mind with 'a corresponding awakening of the soul' without which the development of the mind and the body would become lop-sided. Moreover, education should be for the benefit of society, as only education could churn out socially conscious and responsible men and women. As mere intellectual training could make a person individualistic, socially relevant education along with manual labour would be able to act as an agency of service. Hence, he insisted on team work, discipline, cultivation of a social sense from childhood as the essential ingredients of true education. This education was to be imparted in Indian languages.

At the core of Gandhi's proposal, or the Segaon method as it came to be known, was the introduction of a productive handicraft in the school curriculum which was to be the axis around which the entire teaching programme would revolve. He referred to the humble takli with a view to providing an example of how the entire system of education in the village was to revolve around a particular handicraft. Such a system of education would be inexpensive and also in tune with the needs of the vast rural population. Again, this training in productive handicrafts would ultimately make the schools self-supportive. Gandhi's ideas on village based education amounted to a revolution at that time, as his method entailed a complete all-round education in the village itself, free from the stifling burdens of compulsory English. It was a remarkable modern approach as Krishna Kumar points out, in a crucial way marking a break with India's old concepts of learning.[15]

In October 1937, Gandhi placed his ideas before an educational conference which met at Wardha. The Conference passed the following resolutions:

1. That free and compulsory education should be provided for seven years on a nation-wide scale;
2. That the medium of instruction should be the mother tongue;
3. That the process of education throughout the period should centre around some form of manual and productive work, and all other activities to be developed and training to be given should, as far as possible, be integrally related to the central handicraft, chosen with due regard to the environment of the child; and
4. That the products of the handicraft should gradually be able to cover the remuneration of the teachers.[16]

The Indian National Congress at its Haripura Session endorsed only the first three resolutions. The success of the Basic National Education scheme was dependent on state control.[17] It was in fact, introduced in certain provinces where the Congress had accepted ministries. By 1939, there were 247 basic schools and 14 training schools scattered over nine provinces and states. The Wardha Scheme of education created a stir and stimulated administrators and educationists to think along new lines. The idea was to substitute a co-ordinated training in the use of hand and eye for a notoriously bookish learning which most village children unlearnt after leaving school. The Quit India Movement of 1942, somewhat arrested the progress of this scheme, as most of the members of the *Hindusthani Talimi Sangh* were behind prison bars. While in jail, Gandhi himself devoted much thought to health and education. He spoke not only of Basic education but also of *Nai Talim*. In his expanded vision, education was not merely to be confined to school, but to continue though out life 'from conception to cremation.'

In September 1945, while addressing the New Adult Education Committee Gandhi said, ***"Education for life does not mean education for the duration of life, but education for the sake of life....Adult education is a matter of teaching the art of living. A man who masters the art of living has become a complete human being. Keep this vision before you; let this ideal of Nai Talim inspire your work."***[18]

Gandhi thus had a dream of achieving a silent social revolution through his education programme. He wrote, ***"My plan to impart primary education through the medium of village handicrafts like spinning and carding etc., is thus conceived as the spearhead of a silent social revolution fraught with the most far-reaching consequences."***[19] The object of his basic education was to transform the village children into modern villagers.[20] It was meant to uphold non-violence, and was to be of a non-exploitative character. More importantly, the aim of Gandhian education was not merely to prepare the individual for employment but to make the individuals self–sufficient. For Gandhi the goal of education was character building. He advocated that National Education had a great role to play in the formulation of self-rule. The future of the individual and the progress of the nation were thus wholly dependent upon education. Gandhi never lost sight of the manifold problems and challenges that confronted the nation. His prescription thus envisaged a meaningful, useful and relevant education that would cater to the needs of a post independent Indian society.[21] But Gandhi's vision of providing social justice through the adoption of a village based programme remained unrealized to a large extent as independent India opted to cast its lot with the Macaulayan paradigm.

Notes and References:

1. Easwaran, E. 1983. *Gandhi the Man* [second edition], page 5. UK: Random House Inc [P].

2. Roy, Ranjit Kumar. 1999. *Editorial Note in Modern Historical Studies*, page 1, in *Journal of the Department of History*. Calcutta [India]: Rabindra Bharati.

3. Gandhi, MK. 1938. Educational Reconstruction, page 2. Wardha [India]: Hindusthani Talim Sangh. See also Gandhi's speech at the Wardha Conference on October 22, 1937 quoted in TS Avinashilingam Gandhi's Experiments in Education. 1960. Delhi [India]: Ministry of Education, Government of India.

4. Jain, LC. 2007. *Fate of Gandhi's Economic Thinking* in Sabyasachi Bhattacharya [ed.] *Development of Modern Indian Thought and Social science* [History of Science, Philosophy and Culture in Indian Civilisation Volume X, Part 5], page 22. New Delhi [India]: Oxford University.

5. Gandhi, MK [ed.]. 1937, October 9. *Harijan.* Ahmedabad [India]: HSS.

6. Kumar, Krishna. 1991, Political Agenda of Education: A study of Colonialist and Nationalist Ideas. New Delhi [India]: Sage Publication

7. Ibid, pp.103-24 passim.

8. Ibid, pp.173-4

9. Gandhi, MK [ed.]. 1936, June 11. *Harijan.* Ahmedabad [India]: HSS.

10 Larson, Gerald James. 2011. The Hedgehog and the Fox: Metaphors for the Intellectual Life of Gandhi and Tagore in Pal, Pratapaditya [ed.] *Something Old, Something New in Rabindranath Tagore's 150th Birth Anniversary.* Mumbai [India]: Marg Foundation.

11. Gandhi, MK. 1962. *The Problem of Education,* p. 164. Ahmedabad [India]: Navajivan.

12. Chatterjee, Partha.1995. *Nationalist Thought and the Colonial World,* p. 90. Calcutta: India.

13. Mukherjee, Rudrangshu [ed.]. 1993. *The Penguin Gandhi Reader,* p. 57. New Delhi [India]:Penguin Publishers.

14. Gandhi, MK [ed.]. 1937, September 11. *Harijan.* Ahmedabad [India]: HSS.

15. Kumar, Krishna. 1991. *Political Agenda of Education: A Study of Colonialist and Nationalist Ideas,* pp. 171-2. New Delhi [India]: Sage.

16. See proceedings of the All India National Education Conference, Wardha. Educational Reconstruction, page 156.

17 Chakraborty, Rachana. 1997. *Higher Education in Bengal 1919-47 A Study of its Administration and Management,* p. 130. Calcutta [India]: Minerva Associates.

18. Sykes, Marjorie. 1988. *The story of Nai Talim: Fifty Years of Education at Sevagram*, page 51. Wardha, page 51

19. Gandhi, MK [ed.]. 1937, October 9. *Harijan*. Ahmedabad [India]: HSS.

20. Gandhi, MK. 1981. *The Constructive Programme-Its Meaning and Place*, page 18. Ahmedabad: Navajivan publishing House.

21. Veerraju, Gummadi. 1999. Gandhian Philosophy- Its Relevance Today, pp. 100-04. New Delhi [India]: Decent Books.

*****

Part 3
Conflict Resolution

1

Mapping the Prospects of Conflict Resolution through Peace Education in a Nuclearized South Asia

Preeti Sharma and Sanjeev Kumar

Abstract: The peaceful transformation of the society requires the development of the moral imagination which itself is an exercise in compassion, formed by knowledge and compassion as a means of knowing. Considering this the establishment of lasting peace, congenial security environment and imparting permanence to political stability has been a major cause of disquiet in South Asia. The post-colonial history of the region has been frivolously short to pester the historians in a mastodonic manner, but it has been so heavily loaded with an immensely combustive scenario of conflicts that being oblivious to the region's latent but persistent tumult is very much difficult. South Asia is imbued with several subterranean molecular impulses which have proved to be intractable and have factored deeply in pulverizing peace. Notably ethno-cultural dichotomies; socio-economic inequalities and under-development; and geo-political disputes among the States, significantly, the India-Pakistan conflict, are some of the prominent stimulants in this regard. In this context, it may be argued that the nuclearisation of India-Pakistan dyadic equations added a critical dimension to the nature of conflicts in South Asia. Crossing of the nuclear Rubicon by the two sub-continental adversaries, embroiled the region into a quagmire of uncertainties that pushed the prospects of establishing lasting peace into shambles and became semiotic of a dire existential crisis. Hence, conflict resolution and promotion of cooperation among the region's States have attained paramountcy after the overt acquisition of nuclear weapons by India and Pakistan. This urgent need is being continually underscored by the unremitting conflictual character of subcontinental politics manifested by the outbreak of Kargil crisis, the 2001-2002 military impasse and the unbridled recurring acts of insurgency and terrorism. Thus, the significant aspect to be noted here is that despite the presence of nuclear weapons, there has been no end to the spiral of conflicts in which the region is enmeshed. Unlike the cold war adversarial relationship between the US and the USSR which got moderated after the USSR acquired nuclear weapons that deterred the outbreak of any conflict between them, India and Pakistan have been placed at the threshold of conflict, even as both emerged as declared nuclear weapons States. Worst of all, it allowed Pakistan to destabilize the borders by fomenting insurgency and terrorism and with the help of nuclear brinkmanship, enabled it to deter India from resorting to any pre-emptive strikes to counter this ascendancy. This was demonstrated clearly in India's inability to cross the LOC during the Kargil crisis and its incapacity to acquire any strategic benefit after the 2001-2002 military impasses. So, the existence of nuclear weapons in South Asia has hindered the process of conflict resolution by complicating the nature of regional conflicts. In this way, the instance of sub-continental conflicts in the post-nuclearization era tends to contravene the classical theorizing on nuclear deterrence which holds that the prospects of open conflict between two adversaries is reduced in the event of both acquiring nuclear weapons. As the conflict in the region predates its nuclearization, the means for conflict resolution must be explored from a larger politico-historical, socio-economic and psycho-cultural spectrum. This process to a considerable extent holds the key for conflict resolution and stabilization of peace in South Asia. Spreading of awareness regarding the perils of nuclear weapons at various levels of education, may also prove to be a vital instrument in conserving peace in the region.

Introduction

One of the most essential requirements for the smooth and healthy conduct of human beings' social life is the stabilization of the structures and contours of peace. This has become an indispensible phenomenon in the contemporary age of globalization and high rate of modernity characterized by a perennial risk syndrome. The causes of risks in this age are multidimensional and emanate out of diverse sources. Thus, education in this context becomes a critical tool of preservation of peace by virtue of its capacity to impart knowledge regarding the perils of these risks, advantages of abstinence to those activities that are prone to generate those risks, and also indicate the prospects for progress by containing human beings' intractable and recalcitrant behaviour. Education also inculcates values and moral standards among the members of the society which makes the individuals to be empathetic and practice righteousness while dealing with their fellow beings.

In this regard the role of peace education and peace studies assumes primary importance. Any good peace education and peace studies programme in universities and colleges, however, must not merely be limited to the theoretical and conceptual location of the subject of peace and its detriments, but it should also involve an experiential orientation for the students in various aspects of peace action. More precisely, a confluence of theory and experience, should determine the nature of curriculum for a student of peace education. This will further the cause of encouraging active public participation in protection of peace and, protest those fractious forces out to jeopardize it. [Bing, 1989: 48-50] For achieving this task, a strong commitment to peace is an imperative. [Boyer, 1987: 278-9]

So, at the outset, we may begin by stating that ever since civilized humans have begun communicative engagement with each other, two levels of interactions have emerged. They may be termed as lower politics: the phase of constructive interaction or, cooperation, emerging out of commonness of interests and higher politics; the situation of discord and conflict, emanating out of mutual clash of interests. The circumstance of higher politics seems to have engaged human history and over determined their group behaviour for ages, hence making peace a contentious proposition. This has mainly happened, due to the inherent components of human interaction that fountains from their innate nature, like urge for competition, diffidence rising out of fear of others and love for glory. Owing to all this, the communicative actions among individuals gets impaired to such an extent that there is a total draining away of empathy and remorse for their fellow beings among them.

Thus, the inherent components of human nature are to be nurtured in a manner so as to facilitate individuals to get themselves out of the encasement of their ontological traits and become accommodative to their fellow beings in a manner as to create a concentric space for all. Education emerges as one crucial process for the purpose of accomplishing this task. It is a process of human interaction organized on the basis of individual's capacity for communicative action and hence it is capable of constructing an organic ensemble that can preserve and promote peace. Hence, it may be argued here that in the age of nuclear wars and fierce ethno-cultural asymmetries, an inextricable liaison between education and peace may be found. Education may act as a tool to make individuals and States refrain from their imprisonment in the conflictual psyche. South Asia, which has had a chequered history of conflict and cooperation, is presently under multiple level stresses of a sub-continental nuclear war, multi-ethnic strife and the perils of left wing insurgency and the resultant violence. So, it is an imperative to investigate into the type of linkages between education and peace, in order to explore the possibility of establishing lasting peace and stability in the region. This assumes added importance in the light of the fact that, the countries of South Asia have failed to properly institutionalize cooperation and concretize peace despite several endeavours.

A Conflict Prone History?

A critical hurdle for conflict resolution and reconciliation is the absence of empathy, and also the deep-seated dislike and antagonism that prevails among human beings. [See Deutsch and Coleman, 2000] In this connection, establishment of lasting peace, a congenial security environment and imparting permanence to political stability has been a major cause of disquiet for the entire globe. This has been such an apparent phenomenon in the context of South Asia that its understanding does not require any kind of in depth elaboration or comprehensive justification. The post-colonial history of the region has been frivolously short to pester the historians in a mastodonic manner, but it has been so heavily loaded with an immensely combustive scenario of conflicts that being oblivious to the region's latent but persistent tumult is very much difficult. It has mainly been because of the fact that most of the countries of the region are undergoing the process of democratization; and to a considerable extent, democratization and peace are inversely related to each other. Democratizing societies tend to be fiercely unstable places because numerous groups are entangled in mutual contestations, largely in pursuance of acquiring greater spaces for exerting their influence upon the society and their quest for obtaining more scope to exercise power.

Hence, violence in their region of location becomes very much an obvious and a quotidian phenomenon. In this context, the devious impact of the process of democratization on peace does not get limited to the internal space of the polities. Rather it perniciously permeates into the external space, hence destabilizing the regional security architecture. Thus, democratization involves the complex intercourse between internal peace and external peace in relation to the democratizing polities, with both feeding upon each other in a vicious cycle. This in the case of South Asia has happened because the issues jeopardizing peace in the region are deeply rooted in the internal space of the polities, but their virulence has a spillover effect outside their boundaries.

For instance, contestations of identity that produces fierce ethno-cultural conflicts, divergent notions of nationhood that may lead to geopolitical disputes like those of Jammu and Kashmir, and the struggle for power and strategic dominance largely engendered by a greed stricken paranoid bureaucratic/military/political complexes, emanate from within and induce external conflicts. Hence, it may be argued that the sources of apocalyptical conflicts in South Asia have been endemic, but the fragility in the intra-regional security architecture, also comforted the fractious intervention of outsiders to induce aberrations. So, the region is imbued with several subterranean molecular impulses which have proved to be intractable and have factored deeply in pulverizing peace and stability.

India-Pakistan animosity that possesses all the fractious qualities mentioned above is an archetypical manifestation of the atrocious nature of South Asian conflicts. It has over determined all other consideration when we get down making an analysis of the causes for the enfeeblement of the regional security architecture of South Asia. A deeper look into India Pakistan hostilities also provides pertinent explanation as to the reasons for the predominance of sub-continental dynamics over South Asian regional affairs. If we problematize South Asian security from the perspective of the security dynamics of the Indian subcontinent, May 1998 emerges out as a watershed in this regard.

This is mainly because at this juncture, both sub-continental adversaries lifted the shroud of ambiguity that had cloaked their nuclear postures, after which the entire regional security architecture has come under the constant threat of massive destabilization. The key inducement to this effect is the unremitting adversarial relationship between India and Pakistan. Owing to this, a continuing fear of a nuclear clash has become a realistic proposition and a perennial source to catalyze this, is the unending cross-border terrorism and the resultant tension over their borders. Terrorism, when fused with *Jihad*, is a lethal combination and the emergence of radical Islamist movements has been a major challenge to the regional security architecture of South Asia. Though Muslims, like others, have multiple identities based upon, race, class, tribe, language and territory, the overemphasis on their Muslimness by the extremist practitioners of Islam puts them in collision course with the State and other communities. The extremist assertions of pan-Islamism predicated upon the concept of *Ummah*, poses a grave threat to the pluralistic order of the region. [Warikoo, 2006: 30-43]

The worst form of such a trend is the anti-modernist religious extremism nurtured by Taliban in Afghanistan, which is a Frankenstein monster that emanated out of United States' negative intellectual exercise. This trans-national menace has penetrated deep into wider global spaces, largely due to the efforts of non-State agencies such as the Al-Qaeda. However, Pakistan has emerged as the key nursing ground for fomenting trans-border Islamist extremism and due to this, the nuclearization of the subcontinent has tended to intensify the security predicament of South Asia in several ways. Firstly, the existence of terror infrastructures in a nuclearized Pakistan augments the threat of nuclear backlash by it in the event of any stringent operations to dismantle the same. Secondly in Pakistan, the ISI, the army, the Islamist extremists have been inter-woven into a vicious ensemble with surreptitious patronage rendered by United States' defence and intelligence agencies and this nexus has been emboldened after Pakistan's overt acquisition of nuclear weapons, thus further excruciating the accomplishment of the said task. Above all, United States' increasing influence in shaping key strands of Pakistan's security in the wake of the US led post 9/11 war on terrorism has been a compound effect in this regard.

Further, owing to these inter-locked propositions, and the increasing illegitimate nuclear commerce nurtured from Pakistan, the chances of terrorists laying their hands on weapons of mass destruction have escalated to manifold proportions. Hence, the rapidity with which the pervasive impact of Islamic extremism and the ghastly nuclear competition underway in the subcontinent prognosticates towards a denouement that could be no less than a dooms day for the region. Thus, the advent of nuclear weapons competition, covertly in the 1980s and early 1990s and, overtly after 1998, coupled with violence, terrorism and religious hatred, seems to have destabilized the entire region. This scenario also seems to have mocked the notions of deterrence theorists that the existence of nuclear weapons qualitatively contributes in dissolving conflictual situations. The region after coming under the vicious orbit of nuclear weapons is beleaguered by the fears of inadvertent escalation of any conflict to the nuclear threshold, unauthorized use of nuclear weapons, access to weapons by the terrorists and nuclear accidents. So, nuclearization of South Asia has not only been a detrimental factor for regional security architecture of South Asia, but the prospects of finding amicable solution to long-standing disputes of the region has also become complex.

All this has happened primarily because peace talks, confidence building measures, intervention of multilateral institutions and initiatives towards constructive engagement, have proved to be a parody in South Asia under the constant threat of nuclear weapons and terrorism. So, innovative tools and methods for institutionalizing peace and crystallization of stability should be unravelled. Education, manifested in different forms, may act as a vital tool in this regard. New methods, such as peace and dialogue workshops among two adversarial groups; seminars and conferences represented by members of contending groups; symposiums; contact programmes, etc., may go a long way in providing fecundity to human thinking and imagination, which in turn will shove away their impulse to engage in conflict. The main benefit of these educational instruments is that they impart awareness, build empathy towards the adversaries, and also attenuate the sharpness of antagonism towards the rivals. In a similar kind of peace workshop organized in Sri Lanka among the two rival ethnic groups of the Island nation, it was found that the participants developed an unprecedented sense of empathy for the members of the opponent ethnic group. It was also found that through this contact programme, the antagonisms between them were also considerably reduced. [See Malhotra and Liyanage, 2005] A discussion of South Asian security dynamics in this regard must be based upon the cannons of positivist social science, with strong grounding in novel historical analysis. The contention here must be that conflict resolution, rather than conflict management has become an urgent imperative for preserving the security and stability of South Asia and in this process, peace education may play a significant role.

The Nature of Conflicts in South Asia

When we attempt to understand the problems of peace and the nature of conflicts in a nuclearized security environment, the instance of cold war confrontation between the US and the USSR and, post-cold war sub-continental hostilities between India and Pakistan, present themselves as two asymmetric propositions. If one generated the belief that nuclear weapons deter two adversaries from fighting with one another, the other contested the foundations of this cognition and has tended to reflect antithetical notions to this belief. The theories of nuclear deterrence that emerged during the height of cold war, basically aimed at arguing that there occurred a reduction of tension between the two cold war adversaries, mainly due to the presence of nuclear weapons in the arsenals on both sides. However, there has been a plethora of historical instances of deterrence failures in which non-nuclear States and movements attacked nuclear States, often succeeding in their political objectives. In this regard, the failure of deterrence may occur due to structural cause like the lack of offence-defence distinction, strategic aspect of the stability-instability paradox, cognitive factors, such as misperception and miscommunication, and organizational components like military-organizational pathologies. [Bajpai, 1999: 250-90]

So, nuclear deterrence is not a monolithic conception and varied patterns of its manifestation may be witnessed. The sub-continental nuclear situation is one such unique instance and is far apart from that of the cold war deterrence situation of the US and the USSR. It totally contradicts the notion of nuclear deterrence as there has been no substantial diminution of conflict in the region after the overt acquisition of nuclear weapons by India and Pakistan. Rather, the prospects of the continuation of conflict have been enhanced, hence creating a phenomenological challenge to deterrence theorists. More significantly, the domestic environment in the polities of the sub-continent largely differs from that of the cold war rivals which in itself contributes to the asymmetric notions of nuclear deterrence.

The pressures of local geographical proximity adjacency are also potent for security because many threats travel more easily over short distances than long ones. [Buzan and Waever, 2003: 45] Yet another dimension is that deterrence theories developed during the period of cold war are embedded in the framework of the realist and neo-realist theory of international relations which, in turn, is structured in accordance to the Western notions of Westphalian system of States. Therein, international system is characterized by anarchy generated by the struggle for power among the States, with the impact of the nature and structure of those polities' internal spheres upon their international relations is considered to be inconsequential.

The basic inadequacy of the deterrence theories and the realist and neo-realist theories is their Eurocentricism that limits their capacity to render comprehensive explanation to the nature of the international sub-systems formed by different regions. Their meta interpretations of the world-order based upon the dominant politico-historical discourses shaped by Western experiences, fails to explain the diversities that characterize the regional sub-structures. These regional diversities are carved out of distinct notions of nationhood, multiplicity of ethno-cultural leanings and distinct geo-demographic patterns that impart exclusivity in determining the identity of different regions.

In this perspective, each region must be visualized with a microcosmic approach. Besides, the international system for regions like South Asia, situated in the third world, unlike that of the West is characterized by hierarchy than anarchy, and their domestic space is characterized by anarchy rather than well-defined hierarchy. Third world countries face a world in which informal hierarchal realities severely restrict their freedom of action. It also generates systemic pressures upon them to fashion their behaviour that complies with the interests of the powerful States. Conversely, the domestic politics of the third world is more prone to anarchy due to lack of uniform rules because of the severe constraints of rulemaking amidst highly contending forces. Owing to all this, the State in the third world countries cannot be considered to be modelled on Westphalian lines that is, a State with inviolable boundaries, a monopoly for the use of force in those boundaries and effective democratic governance. [See Ayoob, 1998; Acharya, 1998; and Escude, 1998]

On the other hand, States of the region like South Asia are democratizing, with the process of State construction still in the nascence. This inevitably results in violence, as most of them recently emerged out of colonial fetters and are divided on the basis of diverse linguistic, cultural and tribal identities. It has also to be noted here that in the last part of the Twentieth Century and at the dawn of the new millennium, there has been the globalization of South Asian security dynamics. This has been epitomized by the growing interference of outside powers in fashioning the geopolitical template of the region. At the outset, the magnifying disquiet over the prospects of nuclear war between the two sub-continental rivals has brought in greater global activism in order to diffuse the tensions between them.

United States' security presence has been deep and pervasive in Pakistan, Afghanistan and some Central Asian countries, owing to the war on terrorism. Apart from this, the Anglo-American dyad has also aided the governments of Sri Lanka and Nepal in their endeavours at dealing with civil wars in their polities. Besides this, Norway has also been actively involved in finding amicable ways to resolve the ethnic impasse in Sri Lanka, and Britain has led the international initiatives to deal with the Nepalese quagmire. All this led to the erosion of the strategic autonomy of the countries of the region and made them a prey to the global systemic pressures. Thus, South Asian security dynamics have been globalized under the aura of rampant spread of different forms of anti-regime activities that intensified the fear of widespread State failure and the presence of nuclear weapons raised the vulnerability of the region to such tendencies to enormous proportions.

Hence, to understand the nature of conflicts in South Asia, that too, in the context of a nuclearized security environment, we need to go beyond epistemological debates and develop methods of dialogical analysis which would suit the unravelling of the complex issues involved in shaping the fabric of South Asian security dynamics. The approach must be innovative in so far as to go beyond the Western envisionment of the world system that is done in a manner as to suit the hegemonization of international relations scholarship into a Western mode. One way of understanding the nature of South Asian conflicts is to go beyond the deterrence theories and the realist and neo-realist approach and situate our cognition from the perspective of the conceptualization of *Subaltern Realism' developed by Mohammed Ayoob*. Unlike the realist and the neo-realist approaches to international politics that entirely reject the influence of domestic sphere of polities in fashioning the contours of international system, subaltern realism contends that the aggravation of international conflicts is the extension of the proliferation of internal conflicts in States that has been engendered by the excruciating processes of State construction and its adverse impact such as the crises of governability and even State failure. The process of State construction is inextricably linked with the geo-political geometry of the region and also global power equations. Thus, domestic tumult always tends to be exported to the realm of international politics. Such export takes place because regional balance of power and conflictual scenario are perceived by the State elites as crucial for their State building enterprise. [Ayoob, 1998: 42-3] In this context, Ayoob considers the partition of the Indian sub-continent, the British exit and the mass exodus thereafter, as critical sub-structural propositions in determining the post-colonial India-Pakistan conflict.

Another way of dealing with the issue is to visualize it from the perspective of the theory of Regional Security Sub-Systems or Complexes [RSCs], put forth by Barry Buzan and Ole Waever. This theory argues for the conceptual recognization of the regional security sub-systems or complexes as an intermediate level between global dynamics and internal dynamics that comprised the security relations between local sub-systemic States. For a comprehensive understanding of the regional security sub-system or complex, historical dynamics of amity and enmity must be considered in addition to the regional equations of power which is only partly related to the balance of power. RSCs are defined by durable patterns of amity and enmity taking the form of sub-global coherent patterns of security inter-dependence. [Buzan and Waever 2003: 43-44] Another significant factor is that external actors have little impact upon the historical patterns of amity and enmity and then they do on the distribution of power. Indeed, they tend to acquiesce in local patterns of amity and enmity. The specific patterns of who fears whom and who likes that are not generated by the system level and are generated internally within the region by a mixture of history, politics and material conditions. [Ibid: 47]

Besides this, an important thing to be reckoned with is to look at the conundrum through the perspective of the concept of *culture of peace*, promoted by the United States. This approach was evolved in the programme of action developed by the UN General Assembly [through UN Resolution a/53/

243], to build a culture of peace among the worlds' children. It went beyond the conceptualization of negative peace, reflected in the absence of war, civil disturbances and murder. On the other hand, it envisaged the positive peace of justice, tolerance and plenty. [De Rivera, 2004] This advocacy may act as an educational tool to create certain normative standards, to be emulated by the polities and groups in conflict which would in turn bolster the foundations of regional peace in South Asia. Viewing from this perspective, the conflictual situation in South Asia must be examined in the light of the absence of what has been called as the *culture of peace* and the need to inculcate it through a comprehensive curriculum on peace education at all levels of educational system. So, a broad consideration of the chequered mosaic of South Asian geopolitics, leads us to ruminate over some of the dominant themes that have tended to capture our attention. They include, independence and nationalism, the subtle but intricate linkages between religion and State, the complex linkages between globalization and nuclearization of regional security, the over determinism of the sub-continental dynamics over the entire gamut of South Asian affairs, and most crucial being the lack of a comprehensive model of education that embodies the principles of peace education.

Considered historically, an epochal assessment of pre-colonial and colonial context of South Asia indicates that the geo-politics of the region was largely determined by the nature and structural dynamics of the Indian subcontinent. Moreover, the post-colonial transformations of the regional dynamics do not tend to deviate from this trend pattern. The region has not been entirely dismantled from its historical legacies and despite systemic alterations in the political map of the region, socio-cultural variables impacting upon the models of the politico-strategic and economic architectures are still mired in the past.

South Asian history, in this regard, must be viewed as a montage and the contemporary developments in the region do not seem to demonstrate a marked departure from its earlier patterns. So the sub-continent appears to act as a microcosmic representation of the entire politico-strategic, socio-cultural, psychological and economic processes of the region. Thus, the tantalization of the regional dynamics into an archetypical phenomenon tailored under the geo-political and cultural influence of one of its particular portion is an idiosyncrasy of its own kind. Such omnibus influence of the sub-continental dynamics upon South Asia may be comprehended by examining the effects of sub-continental security paradoxes upon broader paradigm of South Asian security. In this connection, an evaluation of the wider regional impact of various aspects of sub-continental security, which has unfolded in the region's short history, may be done.

Visualizing in these lines, the partition of the Indian sub-continent and the resultant communal holocaust, symbolized the ignition of a tumultuous phase that seems to be timeless in character. The polarization between Hindus and Muslims in undivided India occurred, not so much because of irreconcilable incongruities or deep-seated animosities but merely because of irritants and apprehensions which the minority community suffered. It was largely psychological. Minority groups in all societies perceive a threat and are anxious to preserve their separate identity and culture. Whether such perceptions by the

Indian Muslims are real or imagined is immaterial. Fears can be genuine without being well-based. What is important is that the Muslims harboured such anxieties and the majority communities, or their leaders did little to disarm them. [Rizwi, 1986a: 94]

So, the effects of the tempest that was actuated by the post-partition pogrom and large scale demographic shifts, have been experienced intermittently in the form of destructive wars thanks to the unending politico-strategic rivalry between India and Pakistan. The standardization of this kind of security instability reached grave proportions after the paranoid strategic competition between India and Pakistan, assumed the nuclear dimension. In this context, it may be argued that the nuclearization of India Pakistan dyadic equations added a critical dimension to the nature of conflicts in South Asia. Crossing of the nuclear rubicon by the two sub-continental adversaries, embroiled the region into a quagmire of uncertainties that pushed the prospects of establishing lasting peace into shambles and became symiotic of a dire existential crisis. The mirror images of such probable security instabilities were witnessed during the Kargil crisis and the 2001-2 military impasses between India and Pakistan. Such turmoil always keeps the region at the edge of a potential mass destruction and hampers socio-economic development of the region because the populous seems to be continually angst for a safe and peaceful survival.

The Governments on both sides of the sub-continental divide have also played a devious role in accentuating the hostilities, by the endeavour of promoting their ideologies, programmes and agenda through the means of education. By fabricating historical facts in school text-books, both Governments have vitiated young minds which have had a long lasting ramification upon their psyche. This intensifies the sense of hatred and rivalry among the common public, further excruciating the peace building endeavours. So education, when assumes a perverted form, can be a perilous instrument to induce fragmentations among human beings. This brings to the fore, the need for recognizing the positive role of education in peace making process. If educational processes moves in the proper direction, without being victimized by the Government and the dominant groups of the society, their role in conflict resolution may become definitive. So, it is very important for the Governments of India and Pakistan to realize this aspect, in order to find lasting solutions for their disputes.

Pakistan Factor and India's National Security Dilemmas

Right from the time of India's independence and the creation of Pakistan, South Asia assumed prominent place in the global political cartography, largely for unpropitious causes. The region which was imbued with latent sources capable of inflicting large scale catastrophe even during the colonial era got transformed into a tinderbox in the post-colonial epoch. With the sub-continent getting cleaved into two hostile neighbours, foundations were laid for a tumultuous phase of regional conflicts that has tended to be unremitting. Thus, the inherent fragility of South Asian regional security architecture has largely been fostered by the fierce bilateral rivalry between India and Pakistan. The region's environment has largely been regulated by the temperature of relations between these two sub-continental adversaries primarily because both are embroiled in antagonistic relations for the last more than six decades, the ghastly effect of which has been the nuclearization of the region's security environment.

The complexities of the situation have been acute because all the endeavours at creating concrete peace in the sub-continent have resulted in futility. With India and Pakistan, having fought three major wars till the 1970s, twice being at the threshold of war in the 1980s, engaged in a limited localized war in the 1990s, and almost coming to the brink of a devastating nuclear war recently, the chances of destabilization of the regional security environment have been a persistent phenomenon all through the region's history. Hence, the problems and prospects related to the region's security basically revolve around the nature of the sub-continental security environment.

The historical antecedents of India Pakistan hostilities are varied and complex. The persistence of their adversarial relations till date, that too after several wars and agreements for peace, is a testimony to this phenomenon. To understand this trend, merely historical analysis would be insufficient. A broad sociological and psycho-cultural examination of the deeply embedded dominant factors which are not merely rooted in material structures and go beyond usual cannons of geopolitics must be reckoned with. Hence, the wider cosmologies of India-Pakistan adversarial interactions, begs the necessity of viewing it from the constructivist approach to discern the non-material components such as the divergent notions of identity, nationhood, patterns of the social order predicated upon the social agencies of beliefs, norms and cultural practices.

In this vein, the under-currents stimulating Indo-Pak rift which were largely engendered by the hasty and sloppy process of decolonization, falls into the following broad rubrics. First is the geo-political factor, primarily emanating out of the Westphalian conception of the State that has locked the two neighbours in a state of unremitting hostilities regarding their claims over the territory of Jammu and Kashmir. Territorial conflicts are not merely geographic in character; rather they reflect political tensions derived out of history. [Buzan and Ole, 2003] In this sense the perceptions of both spills into divergent streams. For India, the idea of conceding any territory like that of Jammu and Kashmir to Pakistan amounted to the engendering of the fear of State disintegration. Pakistan, on its part, considered the accession of the disputed territory, as an imperative to complete the process of the geo-political construction of the nation-State on the lines of the historical logic of the two nation theory [Hasan, 1997: 9] which clearly explains the reasons for its irredentist policy in this regard.

Secondly, there existed ideological undertones to this political conflict. It manifested in the divergent affirmations of secularism and Islamic nationhood in the context of Jammu and Kashmir by India and Pakistan respectively. For India, the existence of this Muslim majority territory in the union was essential for providing credence to its nationalist ideology, which contended that all minorities could live safely and progress under a secular pluralist State. The Pakistani ideology, on the other hand, which was largely predicated upon the conception of Islamic nationhood and the idea of Pakistan which was conceived as the homeland for the Muslims of South Asia, could not imagine the completeness of the process of State construction until the Muslim majority Jammu and Kashmir formed part of its political territoriality. In this sense, both India and Pakistan pose systemic threats to each other. India's secular claim over Kashmir within the spirit of a secular federal multicultural polity, challenges the two nation theory and due to this, Pakistan is threatened with dismemberment. On the other hand, Pakistan's sub-continental Muslim nationalism based upon the ideology of pan-Islamism and the two nation theory is a peril for India's federal structure, geopolitical security of Jammu and Kashmir and its multicultural edifice.

Clipped to this, are the dichotomous notions on both sides of the border regarding the conception of nation. Nationhood forms a significant component of identity construction and in this regard, the interpretations of group identities fall into three categories. The primordialist interpretation of the nation sees it as a product of the natural order and the modernist conceptualization of the nation views it as a recent construction, arising from the socio-economic transformation of the past two centuries. The third interpretation is that of the perennialist which tends to understand nationalism as being rooted in long standing ethnic allegiances. [Talbot, 2000: 22-3]

In the subcontinent, nationhood and nationalism, formed significant foundations for identity construction during the period of colonial subjugation. It became the key intellectual tool to contest the dominance of British rule and conceive a collective identity outside the hegemonic ambit of the imperial rule. However, two divergent strands of nation and nationalism emerged during this course. The Indian nationalist movement led by the Congress, attempted at emulating the experiences of the processes of Western modernity and envisaged a nation based upon the principles of the secularization of politics and liberal democratic governance. For the Congress, India represented the collective identity of all the populous irrespective of religio-civilizational differences, who sought liberation from the British colonial yoke. In this way, India as a nation was conceived as an alternative cultural construction to counter the forceful intrusion of British imperial power. This cultural assertion was done by re-inventing the traditional symbols and practices by mating it with the experiences gained out of the exposure to Western cultural practices. This imparted a modernist and a neo-traditional character to it. [See Hobsbawm, 1983] Nation for the Congress, thus, was a kind of 'imagined community' [Anderson, 1983] that was to be knit on the foundations of the fixity of political territoriality and the values of metropolitan governance.

Diametric to this modernist notion of nationhood was the conception of Pakistan which was a homeland for the Muslims of South Asia. Here, the concept of nation implied towards a collective identity based on religious affiliation, that is Islam. The Muslim league which launched a parallel movement for Pakistan with the Indian nationalist struggle, promoted the idea of sub-continental Muslim nationalism, in order to create a collective identity separate from that of India. This divergent conception of nationhood is rooted in the primordialist notions of the nation according to which Islamic nationalism is inherently natural for the followers of Islam that should be expressed in concrete geopolitical terms. Besides, this sense of nationhood is also perennialist as nationalism here is supposed to be rooted in the long-standing ethnic allegiances; which are to say that identity should be conceived in terms of Muslimness.

Thirdly, the realist aspirations on both sides for acquisition of power and regional hegemony tend to keep them entangled in an adversarial posture towards each other. Fourthly, certain structural factors on both sides such as the army and the Inter-Services Intelligence in Pakistan and the *bureaucratic-military complex* in India have emerged as the dominant class in the respective polities with their power interests and have fractiously intervened in keeping the flames of conflict kindled in the region. Broadly speaking, the underlying sources of Indo-Pak conflicts include: power asymmetry, territorial and border problems, differences over nation building strategies and ethno-cultural strife and their international fallout. [Bajpai and Cohen, 1990] Hence, owing to all this, the Pakistan factor has assumed enormous significance in India's foreign policy calculus. An ontologically conflictual relation with it, parochialized India's national security paradigm to the sub-continent, and the nuclearization of the security of both has intensified India's national security dilemmas.

Thus, tumultuous neighbourhood coupled with disputed borders has been a major concern for India's policy-makers. Although the discourse relating to security studies has undergone drastic changes, in the case of India the winds of this change seems to have not touched it. During the period of cold war, the term security was defined by Western intellectuals and practitioners of Statecraft as national security and threatening others. [Dalby, 1988: 415] In this sense, the military dominated conception of national security, that engrossed the entire discourse of security studies during the cold war, required the construction of the notion of a potential threat to identity and political stability of the polity. [Chaturvedi, 1998: 702] In the post-cold war era, however, competing visions of security have been articulated, and the conventional discourses have been subjected to inter-disciplinary scrutiny. [Agnew and Corbridge, 1993: 267] But irrespective of systemic global transformations, India's national security concerns have remained monolithic in character. That means, Pakistan factor has dominated the shaping of the country's national security paradigm since independence and it continues to do so even today.

So, regional security threats, thus, have largely determined India's national security paradigm and also brought the nuclear dimension to its security considerations. [Tellis, 2001: 12] This phenomenon then, brings to the fore, the significance of understanding Pakistan as a key factor in shaping India's national security policy. It has not only been the main security obligation that has preoccupied the thinking and imagination of the policy-makers in India, but has existed as the greatest threat to its external and internal security. [Budania, 2001: 5] Hence, the omnibus presence of the Pakistan factor in India's strategic calculus and foreign policy perception cannot be rebuffed. Both in theory and in the view of the successive Governments, India's security and defence policies have been depicted as holistic and security specific. However, in practice the excessive role of the Pakistan factor in their evolution has made them look very much Pakistan-centric. [Ibid]

South Asia's Tryst with Nuclearization

India-Pakistan belligerence became more adverse, as it got

infected by the germs of the Cold War, after Pakistan joined United States sponsored military block in 1953. It thus facilitated Pakistan to receive massive military assistance from the United States. Compulsions of national security forced India to upgrade its defence capability, in order to counter this Pakistani ascendancy. All this resulted in the germination of an arms race between the two that subsequently transformed into a competition for acquiring nuclear weapons capability.

Further, China factored deeply in India's security considerations and largely determined the alterations in its nuclear policy. India's policy of nuclear abstinence underwent a definitive change, after the first Chinese nuclear test in 1964. This shift in India's nuclear policy to nuclear ambiguity began with its own nuclear test in 1974, which was a watershed in India's nuclear decision-making. [Poulose, 1996: 44] The reasons for the 1974 nuclear tests are varied in character. Firstly, domestic political factors, such as the urge to shore up Indira Gandhi's and Congress party's slipping popularity, coincided by the maturing of the technological progress formed a strong impetus to the 1974 nuclear tests. [Bidwai and Vanaik, 2000: 218-20] The trauma of defeat at the hands of China in 1962 persistently beleaguered the Indian political class and hence, national security threats were naturally inflated after the nuclearization of China. Here lie the roots of India's quest for acquiring nuclear weapons capability which induced the tests.

So, security, rather than international status, was the driving force behind India's nuclear programme. [Singh, 1998: 9-10 and 24-5] Domestic pressures and ideological forces also played a significant role in this regard. The influence of the strategic enclave of scientists and key policy-makers; and Nehruvian State's and Indian elites' desires for symbols and accoutrements of modernity and power, are some other incitements to this effect. [See Abraham, 1998]

However, the weak, indecisive and regionally limited policies resulted in retarding of the further development of nuclear programme which resulted in a twenty four year gap between the two tests. [See Karnad, 2002] Even post-1998, the problem remains the same. The inadequacies of India's nuclear doctrine, uncertainty over the issue of command and control, improper development of the technology to mate the nuclear weapons with delivery systems like the ballistic missiles. Worst of all, the Pakistan-centric character of India's nuclear weapons programme is yet another problem. In fact, India's nuclear programme right from its inception was largely shaped by global forces and to a considerable extent, presence of a nuclear China played its own part. However, off late, India's nuclear programme has tapered down to merely reflecting concerns over security against a nuclear armed Pakistan. Mainly because India existed without any wars with a nuclear powered China and has been constantly engaged in a conflictual relationship with Pakistan. But this long peace with China may not remain in perpetuity. The realist aspirations of China, with an unsettled border dispute with India, may always be a security threat to South Asia. In this regard, the ambiguity over India's second strike capability *vis-à-vis* China raises serious concerns for sub-continental security in particular and South Asian security at large.

On the other hand, India's quest for nuclear weapons

capability emerged as a major challenge for the Pakistani strategists, significantly because India haunts the psyche of the Pakistani ruling elite in the same manner as China does for India. India's military engagement with Pakistan in 1971 and the resultant dismemberment of East Pakistan had a catalytic impact in this regard. Hence, acquiring military parity with India became the sole national objective for Pakistan. This paranoiac urge for parity and the megalomaniacal fantasies of the Pakistani political class, pressed it towards exploring avenues for attaining nuclear weapons capability. Acquisition of nuclear weapons became an epitome of national pride. Zulfikar Ali Bhutto, the progenitor of Pakistan's nuclear program, jingoistically proclaimed, ***"If India developed an atomic bomb, we too will develop one. Even if we have to eat grass, leaves, or to remain hungry, because there is no conventional alternative to the atomic bomb."*** [Bhutto, 1970: 21] So, immediately after the 1971 defeat, Bhutto Government in Pakistan took the decision in pursuance of developing nuclear weapons in January 1972. [Subrahmanyam, 1990: 126] Consequently, a covert nuclear competition began between the two sub-continental rivals that ultimately culminated in their overt nuclearization in 1998.

India's Overt Nuclear Weaponization

Pokhran second nuclear testing of 1998 was the first major policy-decision of the nascent BJP led coalition Government that was related to national security. Not only that, it was an epoch making decision in the history of India as it trumpeted the overt acquisition of nuclear weapons capability by the country. The motives for the tests were candidly spelt out, in the statements from official quarters. The Government was unambiguous in articulating that the aim of this nuclear test was to portray India's credentials as a nuclear weapons power. It was also made amply clear that the tests were conducted, under the compulsions of the prevailing nuclear environment. The Government vindicated the tests by stating that they ***"were not directed against any country and were meant to provide a credible option to counter the geo-strategic threats in the region."*** [*The Hindu*, 1998]

Thus, the prime motive driving India towards open declaration of nuclear weapons capacity has been the requirement of strategic might to fashion the regional security dynamics and hegemonize the regional security system by annihilating any potential threat to its regional strategic supremacy. Historically viewed, India's nuclear weapons programme has been factored deeply in diverse circumstances. Firstly, domestic determinants like the influence of personalities such as Bhabha and Nehru have been as important as that of external security threats. Apart from the domestic State structures and politics, there is also a non-neorealist second image explanation to the issue. In the sense, the nuclear programme has also been attributed to psychological factors, such as the paranoia of racist colonialism and fantasy of obtaining major power status. [Perkovich, 2000: 444-5]

India's policy of maintaining deliberate nuclear ambiguity was largely because of the benign security environment of the region that it confronted in the early years. [Tellis, 2001: 12] So, although the origins of the nuclear programme were non-military, it acquired a military dimension owing to the changing regional and global security systems. But weak political leadership, ad-hoc and incoherent policy-making structures, and a penchant towards legalism and moralism, retarded the process of militarization of the nuclear capacity to reach its logical culmination. The 1998 nuclear tests was, in one respect, a reaction to the indefinite extension of the Nuclear Non-proliferation Treaty and the growing pressures of the US on India to sign the Comprehensive Test Ban Treaty [CTBT] that would have closed India's nuclear option. It was also to a considerable extent, the product of philosophy of the Bharatiya Janata Party. [Kapur, 2001: 203-14]

So, India's nuclear behaviour pattern in recent past has been governed by a combination of three factors: security against China and Pakistan; a search for international status and; acting as a strong domestic determinant has been the electoral commitments of the Bharatiya Janata Party. [Ganguli and Hagerty, 2005: 120-124] In addition to this, the clandestine nuclear programme of Pakistan and its growing nuclear and missile collaboration with China in the 1980s and 1990s is yet another influence towards a definitive transition in India's nuclear programme. Apropos Pokhran Second, the Ghauri missile test by Pakistan on April 6, 1998 has been seen as an impelling force. Besides this, oppositional nationalism that is a combination of the fear of the enemy and pride in one's nation, tends to construct the national identity and makes strong leaders seek symbols of power. This conceptualization of oppositional nationalism suitably represents BJP's ideology and in this vein, a comparison between the Gaullist nationalism and the French programme and BJP's Hindu nationalism and the Pokhran Second nuclear tests could be drawn. [Hyman, 2002: 139-60]

Pakistan's Response

The underlying motives for Pakistan's reaction to India's nuclear tests *Shakti* are deeply rooted in the historical complexities produced at the time of partition. Its anxieties over India's superiority in terms of regional political geometry and India's brazen affirmations of its desires for the creation of larger space for accomplishing its global ambitions heightened Pakistan's anxieties. Rizvi [1986b] argues that three factors contribute for the national insecurity as a state of mind in Pakistan: a narrow and weakly defined purpose in terms of an Islamic State; the absence of a consensus regarding the evolution of national institutions; and the heterogamous nature of the State. Additionally, a bitter history of wars has contributed significantly in intensifying its security dilemma and signified the question as to how the perceived Indian threat should be countered.

To confront this dilemma, a twin-edged approach of fighting a low intensity conflict by fomenting cross-border terrorism to spread terror on the Indian soil, with the acquisition of nuclear weapons capability acting as a suitable foil to this policy was adopted. Since the 1980s, Pakistan successfully used the nuclear brinkmanship through their covert nuclear capabilities, to deter the chances of India using its conventional capacities to gain supremacy during the brass-tacks crisis and at the time of the outbreak of militancy in Jammu and Kashmir in 1989-90. This, then, braced the conviction of the Pakistani policy-makers that the best antidote to desensitize India's combat capacity is by acquiring nuclear weapons. So, the aim of Pakistan was to acquire a strategic parity with India, based upon the concept of essential equivalence. The notion of essential equivalence did not mean a quantitative equality of all nuclear forces between the two countries, but being essentially equal to the other. [Nitze, 1979: 48-9] Thus, the prime mover of Pakistan's nuclear programme and the tests of May 1998 was the urge to acquire a deterrent capability *vis-à-vis* India.

Nuclearization of Sub-continental Conflicts

Since the 1970s, prognosis of the potential nuclearization of India-Pakistan conflict was manifest. This manifestation appeared first in Pakistan's defeat in the war of 1971 and the subsequent germination of a hidden motive for countering India's conventional military superiority with nuclear weapons. India's nuclear test of 1974, acted as a catalyst to this effect and its ramifications were visible during 1980s, when the covert presence of nuclear weapons in the subcontinent created serious tensions between the two countries. The testing of nuclear weapons in 1998 brought all this into the open and resulted in the explicit nuclearization of the long-standing bilateral conflict. Thus, in the sub-continent, the post-1998 security scenario has been marked by a crisis prone, brittle nuclear deterrence situation which has experienced strains intermittently due to the continuing low intensity war on Indo-Pak borders, bolstered by terrorism and violence perpetrated by Pakistan based non-State actors. So, the stability of the deterrence situation in a tumultuous security scenario is an imperative for conflict resolution in South Asia.

There are five crises situations to be reckoned with when we examine the impact of nuclearization upon India-Pakistan adversarial relationship and they must be categorized into two broad streams. The instances in the 1980s fall under the phase in which the two sub-continental rivals possessed a de-facto nuclear status and after 1998, the condition of conflict transformed drastically, as both brazenly unveiled their nuclear weapons capabilities. However, all the five crisis situations: the crisis over the fear of an Indian attack over the Cahuta nuclear complex in Pakistan of 1984, the 1986-7 operation Brass-tacks crisis, the May 1990 tension in the Kashmir valley, the Kargil crisis, and the 2001-2 border mobilization after the December 13 terror attack on the Indian Parliament, fall in a single line and must be viewed as a montage. Specifically, in so far as the impact of covert or overt presence of nuclear weapons constituting the quintessential component underlying all these crises situations is concerned.

However, one factor separating the covert and overt phases of sub-continental nuclear scenario is that during the 1980s, covert presence of nuclear weapons was considered to be a deterring phenomenon in averting three crises, that of 1983-4, 1986-7 and 1989-90. These crises situations occurred against an emerging nuclearized security environment in South Asia, but each one stopped short of getting precipitated into a full blown conflict. It is at this juncture that scholars, strategists and policy-makers on both sides of the sub-continental divide, became optimist of the prevalence of a stable deterrence situation in the region. Firstly, in 1983-4, there were persistent reports that India intended to attack Pakistan's nuclear weapons production facilities and Pakistan threatened to retaliate with a similar attack on Indian facilities. [*Nightly News* 1994] In 1986-7, there occurred a crisis when India conducted its biggest military exercise named Operation Brass-tacks near the borders. The latter fearing that this was a preparation for an attack on it launched a defensive operation named Operation Sledgehammer. In reaction, India launched its Operation Trident and the situation reached the threshold of a massive conflict which was fortunately averted without any further damage. It is at the height of this crisis that Pakistan made an apparent admission that it had acquired nuclear weapons capability.

Lastly, the crisis in the Kashmir valley that transpired in the spring of 1990 was the offshoot of Pakistan's biggest military exercise *Zarb-i-Momin* in late 1989. Due to this, insurgency which was being spawned from the camps located in Pakistan, precipitated to unprecedented proportions in the Kashmir valley. Responding to this, India threatened to carry out cross-border attacks in Pakistan to dismantle the terror infrastructures. Considering this as an act of hostility, Pakistan threatened to weaponize its nuclear capability to confront any Indian attack. Fears of escalation to the nuclear threshold brought in the active diplomatic engagement of the US and USSR in order to dilute the crisis situation. By the time the US sent the deputy national security adviser, Robert Gates, to visit India and Pakistan, the crisis had almost reached the stage of resolution. [See Krepon and Faruqee, 1994; Hersh, 1993] These crises were not played out with ready nuclear arsenal, but were all about nuclear weapons. It was the threat of preventing the construction of nuclear weapons by the opponent in 1983-4, there was the threat to build nuclear weapons in 1986-87 and in 1989-90, and it was the threat of nuclear weapons being used in future. In these crises situations, war supposedly did not occur because of the tacit recognition on both sides regarding the surreptitious presence of nuclear weapons capabilities with the opponent. This kind of an opaque nuclear situation has been described in different ways as: non-weaponized deterrence, wherein deterrence is derived by the power of each to construct nuclear weapons quickly. [Perkovich, 1993: 86] Or, recessed deterrence is a situation in which the countries have the capability to build and deliver nuclear weapons, but that capability is not exercised. [Singh, 1993: 66] And, it is also called as existential deterrence which argues that any aggressor would be deterred from attacking if it feared a similar kind of retaliation. In this way, nuclear weapons rather than encouraging wars, helps to secure peace. [Bundy, 1984: 8-9]

But, the post-1998 sub-continental situation entirely metamorphasized and the perceived stability of nuclear deterrence was pushed into shambles. The explicit nuclearization of sub-continental security coerced the entire region into the short fuse of a nuclear conflict. This scenario was demonstrated firstly during the Kargil crisis. The continuity of an irredentist policy by Pakistan even after the nuclearization of the sub-continent resulted in a disturbing expression of conflict in Kargil. In this sense, Pakistan's action in Kargil, marked a clear departure from the earlier three Indo-Pakistani conflicts. Before this had happened, several experts on strategic affairs had contemplated that Pakistan might use the nuclear status as a better bargaining clout to advance its goals in Jammu and Kashmir. [Ganguli, 1995: 328] In addition to this, many important American and other officials had emphasized the enhanced perils of a nuclear war in the region, given its conflict prone history. [Kinzer, 1999] Kargil crisis seems to be the first epitome of such prognostications. The conflict ridiculed the nuclear deterrence framework and was symptomatic of the ugly ramifications of overt declaration of nuclear weapons capabilities. Kargil thus exhibited that the presence of nuclear weapons did not positively contribute in transforming the security competition between the two. [Tellis et. al., 2002: 1]

However, the nuclear dimension was most apparent during the 2001-2 military impasses that resulted out of the terror attack on the Indian Parliament by Pakistan based militant outfits. This event was preceded by a successful terror strike, on Jammu and Kashmir assembly house in Sri Nagar in October. All this, ushered in with one of the most perilous security situations in the chequered history of India-Pakistan relations, only to be retrograded by the diabolic acts of militants in Kaluchak in May 2002. Owing to these developments, the then Indian Prime Minister, AB Vajpayee, went to the extent of declaring that the war on terror had now reached a definitive stage. With Pakistan exhibiting a sense of reticence towards Indian admonitions regarding its involvement in the trail of terrorist attacks, the latter took recourse to military brinkmanship. The result was consternating. Both India and Pakistan ordered the largest mobilization of their armies in 15 years and a million troops on each side of the border were stationed. [Milewski, 2002: 123]

With this impending conflict, the invalidity of the nuclear deterrence framework in Indo-Pak dyadic equations again resurfaced. From this perspective it may be noted that if nuclear deterrence actually worked in the context of the sub-continental conflicts, instability on the Indo-Pak borders would not have intermittently escalated to perilous proportions making the region constantly vulnerable to threats of a nuclear exchange. [Kumar, 2002]

It seems that overt acquisition of nuclear capability by India and Pakistan has brought contrasting ramifications for State behaviour of the two sub-continental adversaries. On the one hand, it appears to have enfeebled India's capacity to initiate even a limited conventional military offensive and on the other hand, it seems to have emboldened Pakistan in the pursuit of more hawkish strategic and foreign policy against India. This is evident by the fact that ***"India had initiated a plan for conventional strikes across the Line of Control to dislodge terrorist infrastructure in 2002"*** [Gupta, 2002: 27-9], which failed to materialize. This happened due to Pakistan's brazen proclamation regarding its intention to use nuclear weapons. ***"In June 2002, Pakistan's ambassador to the United Nations, Munir Akram, cautioned that Pakistan could resort to the use of nuclear weapons even in a conventional conflict if it considers the losses to be unacceptable."*** [Jayaraman, 2002, cited in Sidhu, 2007: 227] So, the two recent instances of conflicts, the Kargil crisis and the 2001-2 pandemonium, makes it clear that nuclear weapons can deter only a nuclear war and not a conventional or sub-conventional war. [Kumar, 2007: 256]

This conjuncture also demonstrated that the nature of crises in the subcontinent had dramatically transformed. In a marked contrast to the earlier instances of conflict where India exhibited capability to affect a decisive end to the sub-continental conflicts, the post-Pokhran strategic scenario has been entirely different. The nature of sub-continental conflict has got complicated to such an extent that it required the outside intervention to fuse the simmering tensions. The 2001-2 crisis has been such instance that was averted primarily by the intervention of the United States. So, nuclear South Asia is a tinderbox and the moderation of tension urgently requires the spread of the knowledge about the benefits of disarmament and a nuclear weapon free region. This would nurture the region's progress and prosperity.

Hence, for the promotion of peace, development, disarmament, and human rights, education becomes crucial. Education regarding these concepts is important to fathom the inter-connections between them. This may be done on the basis of the 'peace-human rights education-development dialectics', defended as crucial with regard to education that must go beyond the mere transmission of knowledge and attempt at involving in the spreading of awareness among the people of the region regarding their social realities, shared histories and common foundations. [See Marks, 1983]

Apart from this, it needs to be realized that any conflict in a nuclear environment, may end up to be a dooms day for the entire humanity. In such a scenario, training of the human minds by inculcating certain social behavioural traits among diverse categories of different nations, aimed at their progressive growth and stimulating mutual understanding among them is important. Most significantly, the goal must also be to educate the youth in the ideals of peace, mutual respect and understanding among the people, and the development in their minds of a consciousness of the fundamental interests common to mankind. This, most crucially, must be related first of all to inhibit the outbreak of a nuclear war. [Nastase, 1983: 393] So, with the advent of nuclear weapons, the significance of peace education has increased to manifold proportions. As the Governments across the world began to realize the perils of a nuclear war, peace education in the wake of the impending nuclear conflict gained greater patronage. Thus, it may also be stated that the chief goal of peace education is to engender a non-violent social change. [Weigert, 1989: 38]

Conclusion

The peaceful transformation of the society requires the development of the moral imagination which itself is an exercise in compassion, formed by knowledge and compassion as a means of knowing. [Hurst, 1986: 275] This conception seems to be the urgent requirement for building peace in a nuclearized South Asia. Besides, history should be a lesson for the two sub-continental adversaries to understand the fact that nuclear arms race would only be an unavailing endeavour in so far as the protection and promotion of national interests through force is concerned. The deterrence situation of the cold war, explicitly displayed as to how nuclear weapons served as potential instruments that deterred direct and all-out conflicts between the two super powers. The presence of nuclear weapons did not facilitate either side for forceful assertions of the spheres of their national interests. Rather, nuclearization enhanced the misperceptions and lack of trust on the two sides, hence vitiating their relations. The sub-continental experience during the phase of nuclear weaponization on its part, demonstrated that the deep-rooted antagonistic relations between India and Pakistan remained untrammelled. As long as the nuclear status of the sub-continental rivals remained covert, it was assumed that a deterrence situation prevailed in the region which successfully averted the three crises situations. The moment this status got explicit, the fragility of this deterrence situation became apparent, with two crises situations almost reaching the threshold of a nuclear confrontation. This epitomizes the limited explanatory capability of classical deterrence theories in imaging nuclear relationships such as that of India and Pakistan.

So, the deterrence theories are deficient in accomplishing the purpose of exploring modes of conflict resolution in South Asia. This is also largely due to the fact that unlike the US and the USSR, the power asymmetry between India and Pakistan is very much manifest which itself factors deeply in accentuating eccentric security situations, mainly owing to the deeper, psycho-cultural antecedents, affecting animosity. Hence, it is essential to view the sub-continental conflict not merely from the perspective of its nuclearization, rather as the conflict in the region predates its nuclearization, the means for conflict resolution must be explored from a larger politico-historical, socio-economic and psycho-cultural spectrum. Anyhow, in military sphere, the process of institutionalizing Confidence Building Measures [CBMs] and managing deterrence between two antagonists can lead to the institutionalization of co-operative security management that stabilizes deterrence and leads to some sort of détente. [Morgan, 2003: 4] This process to a considerable extent holds the key for conflict resolution and stabilization of peace in South Asia. Spreading of awareness regarding the perils of nuclear weapons at various levels of education, may also prove to be a vital instrument in conserving peace in the region.

Bibliography:

- Abraham, Itty. 1998. *The Making of the Indian Atomic Bomb: Science, Secrecy and the Postcolonial State*. New Delhi [India]: Orient Longman.
- Acharya, Amitav. 1998. *Beyond Anarchy: Third World Instability and National Order after the Cold War* in Stephanie G. Neuman [ed.]. *International Relations Theory and the Third World*. London [UK]: Macmillan.
- Agnew, J. and Corbridge S. 1993. *The New Geopolitics: The Dynamics of Geopolitical Disorder* in RJ Johnston and PJ Taylor [eds.]. *A World in Crisis? Geographical Perspectives*, pp. 266-268. Oxford [UK]: Basil Blackwell.
- Anderson, Benedict. 1983. *Imagined Communities*. London [UK]: Verso.
- Ayoob, Mohammed. 1998. *Subaltern Realism: International Relations Meets the Third World* in Stephanie G. Neuman [ed.]. *International Relations and the Third World*. London [UK]: Macmillan.
- Bajpai, Kanti P. and Stephen P. Cohen [eds.]. 1990. *South Asia after Cold War*. Boulder CO [UK]: Westview Press.
- Bajpai, Kanti P. 1999. *The Fallacy of an Indian Deterrent'* in Amitabh Mattoo [ed.]. *India's Nuclear Deterrent: Pokhran II and Beyond*, pp: 250-90. New Delhi [India]: Har-Anand.
- Bhutto, Zulfikar Ali. 1970. *Awakening the Nation: Speeches of Zulfikar Ali Bhutto 1966-1967*. Rawalpindi: Pakistan Publications.
- Bidwai,Praful and Achin Vanaik. 2000. *South Asia on a Short Fuse: Nuclear Polities and the Future of Global Disarmament*. New Delhi [India]: Oxford University Press.
- Bing, Anthony G. 1989, July, *Peace Studies as Experiential Education* in *Annals of the American Academy of Political and Social Sciences* –Volume 504, pp. 48-60

- Boyer, Ernest L. 1987. *College: The Under Graduate Education in America.* New York [USA]: Harper and Row.
- Budania, Rajpal. 2001. *India's National Security Dilemma the Pakistan Factor and India's Policy Response.* New Delhi [India]: Indus.
- Bundy, McGeorge. 1984. *Existential Deterrence and its Consequences* in D. MacLean [ed.]. *The Security Gamble: Deterrence Dilemmas in the Nuclear Age.* Totowa NJ [USA]: Rowman and Allenheld.
- Buzan, Barry and Ole Waever. 2003. *Regions and Powers: The Structure of International Security.* Cambridge [UK]: Cambridge University Press.
- Chaturvedi, Sanjay. 1998. *Common Security? Geopolitics, Development, South Asia and the Indian Ocean* in *Third World Quarterly.* 19[4], pp. 701-24
- Dalby, Simon. 1988. *Geo-Political Discourse: Soviet Union as the Other* in *Alternatives,* Number -13, pp. 415-42
- De Rivera, Joseph. 2004. *Assessing the Base for a Culture of Peace in Contemporary Societies* in *Journal of Peace Research.* 41[6], pp. 531-548
- Deutsch, M. and Coleman, PT [eds.]. 2000. *The Hand Book of Conflict Resolution: Theory and Practice.* San Francisco [USA]: Jossey-Bass.
- Escude, Carlos. 1998. *An Introduction to Peripheral Realism and its implications for the Interstate System: Argentina and the Condor II Missile Project* in Stephanie G. Neuman [ed.] *International Relations Theory and the Third World.* London [UK]: Macmillan.
- Ganguli, Sumit and Devin T. Hegerty. 2005. *Fearful Symmetry: India-Pakistan Crisis in the Shadow of Nuclear Weapons.* New Delhi [India]: Oxford University Press.

- Ganguli, Sumit. 1995. *The Study of Conflict and Terrorism*. 18[4], pp: 325-38
- Gupta, Shishir. 2002. When India Came Close To War'. *India Today*. 23 December, pp: 27-29
- Hasan, Mushirul. 1997. *Introduction to India's Partition Process: Strategy and Mobilization*. New Delhi [India]: Oxford University Press.
- Hersh, Seymour. 1993, March. *On the Nuclear Edge* in *The New Yorker*, Number- 99, pp. 56-73
- Hobsbawm, Eric. 1983. *Inventing the Tradition*. Cambridge [UK]: Cambridge University Press.
- Hurst, John. 1986. *A Pedagogy for Peace. The World Encyclopedia of Peace*. New York [USA]: Pergamon Press.
- Hyman, Jaques. 2002. *Why Do States Acquire Nuclear Weapons?* in DR Sardesai and Raju GC Thomas [eds.] *Nuclear India in the Twenty-First Century*, pp. 139-60. London [UK]: Palgrave Macmillan.
- Jayaraman, T cited in Waheguru Pal Singh Sidhu. 2007. *Operation Vijay and Operation Parakram: A Victory of Theory*? In E Sridharan [ed.]. *The India Pakistan Nuclear Relationship: Theories of Deterrence and International Relations*, pp. 208-38. New Delhi [India]: Routledge.
- Kapur, Ashok. 2001. *Pokhran and Beyond: India's Nuclear Behaviour*. New Delhi [India]: Oxford University Press.
- Karnad, Bharat. 2002. *Nuclear Weapons and India's Security: the Realist Foundations of Strategy*. New Delhi [India]: Macmillan.
- Kinzer, Stephen. 1999, June 9. *Kashmir Gets Scarier* in *The New York Times*.
- Krepon, Michael and M. Faruqee [eds.]. 1994, April. *Conflict Prevention and Confidence Building Measures in South Asia:*

The 1990 Crisis. Occasional Papers Number -17, Washington DC [USA]: Henry L Stimson Center.

- Kumar, Arvind. 2002, August 22. *Nuclear Deterrence: A Waning Motif* in *Deccan Herald* and in *Theories of Deterrence and Nuclear Deterrence in the Subcontinent* by E Sridharan [ed.] as *The India Pakistan Nuclear Relationship: Theories of Deterrence and International Relations*, pp. 239-65. New Delhi [India]: Routledge.
- Malhotra, Deepak and Sumanasiri Liyanage. 2005, December. *Long Term Effects of Peace Workshops in Protracted Conflicts. The Journal of Conflict Resolution*. 49[6], pp. 908-28
- Marks, Stephen. 1983. *Peace, Development, Disarmament and Human Rights Education: The Dilemma between the Status Quo and Curriculum Overload. International Review of Education*, 29[3], pp. 289-310
- Milewski, Pawel. 2002. *'Pakistan India and the Events of September 11*. Polish Quarterly of International Affairs. 11 [4], pp. 1238 Winter.
- Morgan, Patrick M. 2003. *Deterrence Now*. Cambridge: Cambridge University Press.
- Nastase, Adrian. 1983. *The Culture of Peace and Peace Education. International Review of Education*, 29 [3], pp. 391-401
- *Nightly News*. 1994, August 30
- Nitze, Paul H. 1979. *Assuring Strategic Stability in an Era of Détente* in Hanrieder [ed.] *Arms Control and Security: Current Issues*. Boulder CO: West view Press.
- Perkovich, George. 1993. *A Nuclear Third Way in South Asia. Foreign Policy*. Number -91, Summer, pp. 85-104, and 2000. *India's Nuclear Bomb: Impact on Global Proliferation*. New Delhi [India]: Oxford University Press.

- Poulose, TT. 1996. *India's Nuclear Option and National Security* in PR Chari, Parvaiz Iqbal Cheema and Iftekhar Uzzaman [eds.]. *Nuclear Non-Proliferation in India and Pakistan: South Asian Perspectives*, pp. 44-59. New Delhi [India]: Manohar.
- Qadir, Shaukat. 2002, April. *An Analysis of the Kargil Conflict-1999*, pp 24-30. *RUSI Journal*-147 [2].
- Rizvi, Gowher. 1986. *The Rivalry between India and Pakistan* in Barry Buzan and Gowher Rizvi [eds.]. *South Asian Security and the Great Powers*. London [UK]: Macmillan and 1986 *Pakistan: The Domestic Determinants of Security* in Barry Buzan and Gowher Rizvi [eds.] *South Asian Security and the Great Powers.* London [UK]: Macmillan.
- Singh, Jasjit. 1993. [ed.]. *Nuclear Deterrence: Problems and Perspectives in the 1990s*. New York: United Nations Institute for Disarmament Research.
- Singh, Jasjit. 1998. [ed.]. *Nuclear India*. New Delhi: Knowledge World.
- Sridharan, E. 2007. *Subcontinental Perspectives on Deterrence Theory, International Relations Theory and South Asia* in E Sridharan [ed.]. *The India Pakistan Nuclear Relationship: Theories of Deterrence and International Relations*, pp 9-25. New Delhi [India]: Routledge.
- Subrahmanyam, K. 1990. *Security in a Changing World.* New Delhi [India]: BR Publication Corporation.
- Talbot, Ian. 2000. *Inventing the Nation: India and Pakistan.* New York [USA]: Oxford University Press.
- Tellis, Ashley J. 2001. *India's Emerging Nuclear Posture from Recessed Deterrent to Ready Arsenal*. Santa Monica, CA [USA]: Rand.
- Tellis, Ashley, et. al. 2002. *Limited War Conflict under the Nuclear Umbrella: Indian and Pakistani Lessons from the Kargil Crisis.* Santa Monica CA [USA]: Rand.

- *The Hindu*. 1998, 14 May. *Nuclear test not directed towards any country*, page 1. Chennai [India]: THP.
- Warikoo, K. 2006, January-March. *Islamic Extremism: A Challenge to South Asia* in *Strategic Analysis* 30[1], pp. 30-45
- Weigert, Kathleen Mass. 1989, July. *Peace Studies for a Nonviolent Social Change* in *The Annals of the American Academy of Political and Social Science*, Volume -504, pp. 37-47

*****

Part 4
Methodology

1

Gender Perspective on Education and Peace

Vibhuti Patel

Abstract: Peace of course can have two faces, two forms- Public and private. Peace in the community, go hand-in-hand with the peace in the family life. Hence, the need to deal with domestic violence and women's grievances. There may be an apparent stability and absence of conflict in situations of successful intense repression-beating, abuses, psychological torture wherein all dissent is brutally, immediately, and surgically suppressed. This is a condition in which only one group [men, in-laws, bully neighbours] dominates, in which women's views and dignity is not allowed to exist. The other situation is one in which democracy and human rights reach their pinnacle in each and every core of the community and domestic lives. It is the condition in which there are always avenues of settlement of differences and disputes without a breakdown of the framework of mutual respect, recognition of the rights of the other, and belief in good faith of the *adversary*. It is the condition in which negotiations and persuasion are the methods of overcoming even major digressions in points of view. It is a condition in which people have the right to be different and where difference is not denied. It is also the state of affairs in which difference is not a cause of hierarchy, where the other is not the enemy or the lower or the higher being. The quest for peace is an eternal pursuit for human fulfillment. Peace or absence of antagonistic, violent, or destabilizing conflict is essential for existence to become life, for survival to become human. Human beings can become human and humane only in conditions of peace. Creativity, spirituality, individual and collective achievements attain grandeur and glory only when there is peace. Qualities of compassion, forgiveness, love, sharing and universal solidarity become cherished and sought after virtuous attributes only when a community, society or nation is at peace-within and without. War on the other hand, internal or external, civil or military, declared or undeclared valorizes bravery-the capacity to kill or be killed-the destruction of human life and accomplishments; it mocks compassion and conscience; it belittles refusal to erect artificial walls that divide human beings in the name of one identity or the other; it glorifies the destructive principle and devalues the principles of creation and life. The war mongers are invariably persons with few qualms of conscience, ever ready to eliminate and exterminate human life, emotions, thought, ideas, and achievements. In this context, for empowering harmony at the individual and community level, liberal humanism needs to be backed by solidarity, service and authority. Social activists like us have to organize and mobilize men, women and children to reiterate and reinforce the importance of secular values for a harmonious coexistence, to create pressure groups to condemn acts of violence and exclusion and to propagate actions and initiatives to promote peace and inclusion and to encourage, facilitate and establish similar networks/coalition of citizens to promote secular values, religious tolerance, democracy and human rights and accelerate women's participation in secular movements striving for equality and justice. To resolve conflicts with words, rather than swords.

Introduction

When faced with violence, women's predicaments as survivors, as beneficiaries of violence & as peacemakers are extremely complex issues. Women's complicity in perpetrating violence in case of female infanticide, female foeticide, dowry murders, during caste/communal/ ethnic violence and in the war-zones [Abu Grahib prison in Iraq] are widely documented. Thus, the belief that 'women as inherently peace-lover' is contested by the human rights movement. Women are also carriers of culture of violence. At the same time, five thousand years of patriarchal control over women's sexuality fertility and labour makes mass of women victim of violence. Social discrimination against women results into systematic neglect of women's health, from womb to tomb. Sexual assault, molestation, rape, sexual harassment at workplace, child sexual abuse, nuisance calls cause psychological disturbances among girls and women. The trauma of sexual violence sparks off tension and anxiety at a dangerous level. Their mental health problems are manifested in anxiety, fear, avoidance, guilt, loss of efficiency, lack of coordination, depression, sexual dysfunction, substance abuse, relieving the traumatic incidents through memory, suicidal attempts, eating disorders, disturbed sleep patterns, fear of encountering such situation once again. It is found that women who undergo extreme sexual violence experience a loss of self and self-esteem following the shock inflicted on them. When there is a continuous period of traumatic stress, it becomes chronic, lessening the individual's ability to do any kind of constructive work. Hence, this form of male violence towards women is an important issue that demands public attention. Women's organizations have taken up this issue at a local, national and global level. Discourse on mental health of women in the family situation gained serious consideration in the context of campaign against violence against women. In domestic violence situations, predicament of women is determined by their position in power-relations vis-à-vis the rest of the family members. Many social work researches which attribute deviant behaviour of adolescent girls to their working mothers guilt trip women by narrowly focusing on single parameter and ignoring factors such as peer –pressure, media, overall standards of morality in our society and power relations in the nuclear/joint family. Such researches are used by some counselors to cage women into domesticity and divert the attention from generation of genuine support system for developmental needs of the daughters of working mothers. Women's rights organizations which are doing support work for women in distress have started giving due importance to counseling for peace building.

The quest for peace is an eternal pursuit for human fulfillment. Peace or absence of antagonistic, violent, or destabilizing conflict is essential for existence to become life, for survival to become human.

Women as Survivors of Violence and Conflict

Eyes raining, without mere control,
Scruples hurt, thus dew drops roll.

Lightened, piercing, still with grief,
Forever, staring in disbelief.
Hearts melting, defenses down,
Afflicted feelings, all around.
Timeless moments, of unending sorrow,
Darkened scars, that none can borrow.
Deep in hurdles, full with distress,
Pleasures replaced, by pure sadness.
Love's demise, of responsive pain,
A day's repose, then it starts again.

This poem by a survivor of violence and conflict, Ms. Lara Jesani portrays the pain and agony that every woman faced with domestic violence, communal/caste/ethnic violence and violence as a result of war.

Peace Begins from Home...A Case Sturdy of Women's Grievances Cell of Mohalla Committee Movement; the Mumbai Mohalla Committee Movement [MCM] in Mumbai was formed with a firm understanding that the quest for peace is an eternal pursuit for human fulfilment.

The MCMs were formed in Mumbai to counter communal frenzy during Bombay riots in 1992-3. In the words of its founder member Julio Francis Ribeiro, ***"After the riots in Mumbai in 1992, a long term, interventionary and developmental solution was deemed necessary. The creation of Mohalla committees was one of the solutions proffered and their proliferation in various areas of Mumbai has made a measurable difference in the life of this metropolis. These committees were seen as simple, people-centred and appropriate mechanisms through***

which peoples' participation in the peace process is highlighted." The MCM made a crucial contribution to restore peace and confidence among different communities. Moreover, it promoted developmental activities such as education, civic issues and programmes for youth and students. As the MCM has a gender-sensitive approach and does not believe that *women's issues can wait*, it decided to focus on women- both in the community as well as in the domestic arena.

Formation of the Women's Grievance Redressal Cell

Women in the communities have been mainstays of the MCM. Women's response to the proponents of *World Peace* was *Peace begins from home.*

Peace of course can have two faces, two forms- Public and private. Peace in the community, go hand-in-hand with the peace in the family life. Hence, there is the need to deal with domestic violence and women's grievances. There may be an apparent stability and absence of conflict in situations of successful intense repression-beating, abuses, psychological torture wherein all dissent is brutally, immediately, and surgically suppressed. This is a condition in which only one group [men, in-laws, bully neighbours] dominates, in which women's views and dignity is not allowed to exist.

The other situation is one in which democracy and human rights reach their pinnacle in each and every core of the community and domestic lives. It is the condition in which there are always avenues of settlement of differences and disputes without a breakdown of the framework of mutual respect, recognition of the rights of the other, and belief in good faith of the *adversary.* It is the condition in which negotiations and persuasion are the methods of overcoming even major digressions in points of view. It is a condition in which people have the right to be different and where difference is not denied. It is also the state of affairs in which difference is not a cause of hierarchy, where the other is not the enemy or the lower or the higher being.

To create such condition, the MCM initiated a project- the Women's Grievance Redressal Cells [WGRC] in March, 1997, first at the MIDC and on April 2, 1998 in Andheri [East] to enable women of different communities to come together on a common platform.

Distressing Condition of Women in the Community

While working in the community, the MCM activists realized that women were doubly oppressed, both socially and economically and hence needed an outlet to voice their grievances. Most of the women led submissive lives and suffered in silence. Ironically, even though communal harmony prevailed in the area, marital conflicts disturbed the peace and tranquility of the families. Many of them had to face physical violence their personal lives.

Even so they were apprehensive of lodging a complaint at the police station, either out of fear of society or due to fear of retaliation/backlash from the family members, especially husbands. It was in this background that the members of the MCM along with the police conceived the idea of WGRC in order to help women in distress.

These cells made the people aware of a common link

between women and the community they live in. As a result, effective outreach programmes were developed and major extension activities were initiated to promote peace, communal harmony and constructive activities for area development. These cells, being projects of the MCM are working in collaboration with the local police and three NGOs function twice a week at the MIDC and Andheri [East] police stations.

Awe inspiring experiences of these two Cells, motivated the members of the MCM to start similar cells in Bandra, Nagpada and Worli.

Objectives of the WGRC

1. To work with individual women and men, families, groups and communities to create harmonious gender relations and to promote ethos of cultural pluralism;
2. To give the women a listening ear and to take cognizance of the offences perpetrated on them;
3. To coordinate with the police in cases of crimes against women;
4. To conduct training programmes/workshops for women as well as the family members on wide range of issues and themes concerning multicultural existence, developmental problems and skill and capacity enhancing projects;
5. To network with women's organizations and other like-minded organizations for collaborative work; and
6. To facilitate and mediate out of court settlements and if needed, to organize legal services for women at affordable rates.

Approach of the WGRC

As the thrust of the cell is on mediation and reconciliation, all the concerned parties are invited to the cell and given a fair chance to voice their grievances against each other. Some of the meetings can be very time consuming. However in some cases, redressal process is shorter and cases quickly get resolved.

Due to consistent activities of the MCM in the community, the Women's cell could get easily established and legitimized as many women who approached the cell were also the members of the MCM and attended the MCM meetings regularly in their respective beats. The following examples delineate the processual dimension of the WGRC's intervention:

A. Easing of Tension Between Hafeeza Shaikh and Vimal Pawar [MIDC]

For several years, Hafeeza and Vimal were at loggerheads. Even though their fights revolved around issues such as garbage and drainage, their anger and hatred towards each other was immense. Both had lodged complaints and counter complaints against each other at the police station. But to no avail, the animosity between the two continued to prevail. Finally, the duty officer at the police station asked them to visit the WGRC.

On visiting the WGRC, both complained bitterly against each other. While Vimal blamed Hafeeza of witchcraft, Hafeeza blamed Vimal for provoking the fights and instigating the neighbours against her. It was evident that both did not want reconciliation. It was a Herculean task for the members of the cell to bridge the gap between the two as they belonged to two different communities. However, after a continuous dialogue with them at the end of the third session, both agreed to bury the past and forgive each other. The cell members were jubilant as they were able to resolve the problem that existed for many years and most importantly they were able to bring about peace in the area, especially since Hafeeza's was the only family from the minority community living in a majority dominated area.

B. Reformed Swamy and Relieved Vasanthi [Andheri]

Vasanthi, a young girl, married C Swamy in 2003. However, on the very next day of her marriage, her husband demanded money to set up his business. She was shattered. In order to keep her marriage intact, she borrowed a small amount of money from her father and gave it to her husband. Still he continued to harass her mentally and physically for more money. Moreover, he forcibly took her gold ornaments and sold them for a large amount of money. Torture by her husband was so her unbearable that she left her matrimonial home to live with her parents. Her parents felt so cheated by their son-in-law that they decided not to send Vasanthi back and decided to call of the marriage. It was at this point in time that distraught Vasanthi approached the cell and related her woes to the members. Vasanthi's husband was subsequently called to the cell and there was a major showdown between the spouses. The members made uphill effort to seek reconciliation between them. But it was only after the second session that Vasanthi's husband agreed to return the money and jewels and do a service job. After the third meeting both the spouses agreed to give their marriage a try and Vasanthi returned to her husband. They are in touch with the WGRC and the cell members have found that Swamy has changed for better.

Nature of Grievances

In nutshell, there are seven natures of grievances:

1. Marital conflicts [wife-beating, extra-marital relationships, alcoholism, unemployment, financial constraints];
2. Problems concerning in-laws;
3. Disputes with neighbours;
4. Conflicts with kith and kin;
5. Sexual problems [impotency, violent sexual encounter, pervasive and lustful behavior];
6. Love affairs resulting into elopement and marriage; and
7. Divorce, desertion, maintenance, illegal second marriages.

Legal Intervention

The cases that could not be resolved through negotiation were either referred to the family court at Bandra or to individual lawyers. Some women filed their petitions in the family court for maintenance and divorce while others sought the help of their lawyers in connection with illegal marriages, child custody and dowry demands made by their husbands. An advocate from the Tata Institute of Social Sciences [TISS] also helped with her legal expertise at the cell at MIDC.

Teamwork Between the Police and the WGRC Members

In all the cells, the police constables are a part of the team. Their presence helps the WGRC to get a better insight on the problems faced by numerous women and moreover it gives an opportunity to empathize with the victims in need of help. The police also play an important role by visiting the home of the victim and inviting the spouse to the cell for mediation.

Follow-Up Work

The WGRC visits the homes where the conflict is of a serious nature so as to assess the prevailing situation. If the relationship continues to be strained, the spouses are once again invited to the cell for further mediation.

Empowerment of Women Through Human Rights Education

The WGRC believes that public education is the major tool to women's empowerment. Hence, it organized five workshops on gender sensitization at Bandra-Kurla police station for the police personnel of the west region. The team from the legal aid cell of justice and peace commission conducted sessions on The Universal Declaration of Human Rights, laws related to women and crimes against women. The five-day workshop provided legal training to three hundred police personnel that included constables, sub inspectors, inspectors and assistant commissioners of police. Even women police took active part in the workshop that was divided into a lecture, a group exercise and a slide show.

The WGRC has also organized workshop on women and health, counseling, legal provisions, communication skills and unlearning communalism through creative methods of role-play, storytelling, group exercises, street plays, screening of films, vocational training programmes, *haldi kumkum samaroha, rangoli* and poster competitions and teaching precautions like first aid, fire extinguishing skills.

Commemoration of International Women's Day

The Eighth March, the International Women's day, that

symbolizes solidarity, sisterhood and strength of women, has been a focal point for women from all five cells to meet at one place and get a feeling of empowerment. For the past seven years, the cell has been celebrating this day with vigour an enthusiasm reflected in singing of group song, experience sharing, presentation of annual progress report, speeches of dignitaries and children's stage shows. These events have instilled a feeling of confidence and leadership qualities in women.

Pre-emptive Measures

Knitting Communities together has been the most effective tactic for preventing communal conflagration. In 2002, after the communal carnage in Gujarat, there was a lot of tension in the community. The Women Grievance Redressal Cell [WGRC] worked with the police and held meetings all across the city through the MCM. The WGRC also participated in the MCM-organized painting competitions, cultural programmes on communal harmony, sports like volley ball, gymnastics and athletics, table tennis and 'cricket for peace' as friendly and healthy competitions to inculcate a spirit of recreation to counter cut-throatism and promote peace making. After these programmes, many participants have expressed their feelings, ***"Until now we were very scared and prejudiced about the police and did not feel we could approach them. But these past few days have helped us to overcome this."***

Study Rooms

The other strategy implemented by the *Mohalla* Committees has been in the setting up of study rooms, as in many slum colonies young students do not have a quiet space where they can study. Often many of them need help with their studies. By using the classrooms of local municipal schools, which are free and unused in the evenings, the *Mohalla* Committees have been able to provide a much-needed service to their communities.

Twelve Steps [1997-2009] to Women's Empowerment

During the last twelve years of its existence, the WGRC has played an important role in cementing the bonds between communities, spouses, neighbours and enlightened the youth. It is an acknowledged fact that the WGRC has played a useful role in forging a meaningful relationship between individuals in the family and also expanded the meaning of family that encompasses the whole community. At the time of communal tension [at times of religious festivals, release of controversial films depicting inter-religious love marriage, during ongoing unsecular episodes happening elsewhere] both police and the cell members play a proactive role and display courage of conviction to diffuse the tension. This has been possible due to the close and constant co-operation between the police and the *Mohalla* Committees.

The work of the MCM has been successful only in areas where police officers have taken personal interest and have ensured that the right kind of people are inducted in the Committee. After seven years of functioning of the WGRC, both the communities and the police have realized that the process requires constant vigilance and evaluation. The WGRC member are torchbearers of women's dignity, bodily integrity and gender-justice. Activities of the WGRC have brought women's issues on the agenda of the MCM. Now, members in the community accept that women's rights are human rights. This experience of the MCM needs to be replicated throughout the nation.

Women as Beneficiaries of Peace Process

Women are the main beneficiaries of peace process as it allows them freedom of movement and ensures their active participation in education, skill and enterprise development, better health status and in terms of employment and career option.

Even in the midst of massive transformatory processes, women leaders from different parts of globe provided different models of peace building thro' constructive work.

Wangari Muta Maathai, Kenya, Birth 1940 was awarded the Nobel Peace Prize in 2004 for her contribution to sustainable development, democracy and peace. Wangari Muta Maathai was born in Nyeri, Kenya, East Africa in 1940. Prof. Maathai was the first women from East Africa to gain a doctorate. She studied Biology at Kansas and Pittsburgh before attaining her Ph. D. from the University of Nairobi in 1971 [Anatomy]. Prof. Maathai was active in the National Council of Women of Kenya [NCWK] from 1976 to 1987 and it was during this time that she was active in starting a tree planting project to help protect the environment. The Greenbelt Movement was founded by Wangari in 1977, starting with a small tree nursery in her backyard. The movement promotes sustainable livelihoods, citizen education and reforestation, involving mainly women. Millions of trees have been planted in Kenya and other African countries. Over the years, Wangari has opposed Government and others in Kenya over land-grabbing, deforestation and governance issues. In 2002, she won a landslide victory from her home constituency to become a Parliamentarian, and under the new coalition Government was appointed Assistant Minister for Environment, Natural Resources and Wildlife. Wangari is internationally recognized for her persistent struggle for democracy, human rights and responsibility, and environmental conservation. She serves on the boards of several organizations.

To Give Peace a Chance, Make Peace the Story

While reporting every media personality must have faith, ***"In every conflict, there is always something retrievable."*** It is very important to popularize peace journalism. Public felicitations of persons involved in rescue operations and rehabilitation such as nurses of Cama Hospital in the midst of terrorist attack on November 26, 2008 and hundreds of unsung heroes and heroines.

Popularize efforts of global, national and local networks involved in peace-making. For example, The Thousand Cranes Peace Network is made up of groups and individuals who are willing to fold a thousand paper cranes [or as many as they can manage] as a symbol of their hope for, and commitment to, peace and non-violence. A visit to the Peace Park and the Peace Memorial Museum allows the visitor a glimpse into the horror of the world's first use of the atomic bomb against people on August 6, 1945. It is a reminder that we must work together to make sure that such a tragedy never happens again.

Women as Peace Makers

Women have built peaceful movements to fight against excesses of the dictatorial regimes in Philippines, Chile, Bangladesh, Burma, so on and so forth.

Aung San Suu Kyi was born on June 19, 1945 at Rangoon, capital of Burma [now Myanmar]. Her father, Aung San was commander of the Burma Independence Army and was assassinated when she was two years old. Her mother, Daw Khin Kyi was appointed as Burma's ambassador to India during 1960. Suu Kyi accompanied mother to New Delhi and studied at high school and Lady Shri Ram College in New Delhi from 1960 to 1964. Her stay in India instilled in her a deep rooted belief in Gandhian philosophy. In 1964 she left India and studied further in University of Oxford where she met her husband, Dr. Michael Aris, a visiting professor at Harvard University appreciated her leadership of the pro-democracy movement in her country. Her scholarly pursuits took her in subsequent years to United Nations, Kyoto University, Japan and the institute of Advanced Studies, Shimla. In 1988, Aung San Suu Kyi returned to Myanmar to nurse her ailing mother. There the mass slaughter of protesters against the brutal rule of military General Ne Win made her to speak out against him. She began non-violent struggle for democracy and human rights. She affiliated herself with the newly formed group, the National league for Democracy. The League won more than eighty percent of the parliamentary seats in the elections of 1991. However, the results of the election were ignored by the military government. For six years she was placed under house arrest by military rule and offered to release her if she agrees to leave Myanmar. She was ultimately freed from the house arrest in 1995.In recognition of her non-violent struggle for the restoration democracy in Myanmar; she received several prestigious awards including Nobel Peace Prize in 1991. She also received Human Rights Prize in 1991. In 1995, India conferred the Nehru Award for International Understanding on Suu Ki.

Five Priorities for Conflict Resolution and Peace

Practitioners involved in Conflict Resolution are unanimous in their conviction about five core principles and they are:

- Dialogue, communication, networks- the Centre for Studies in Society and Secularism [CSSS], Mumbai has been doing this for past two decades thro' research, documentation, training of people of all stake groups;
- Contemplation-Communalism Combat, [hate-hurts, harmony works] a monthly magazine provides platform for debate and discussion on political economy of conflicts and ways to resolve them;
- Community Life-Moholla Committee Movement is doing illustrious work that must be replicated everywhere;
- Justice, peace and integrity of creation in solidarity with the most vulnerable- JPCs must attract all types of professions; and
- Simple living, solidarity for social/economic justice: All approaches, from A to G advocate socio-economic and gender justice.

Ela Ramesh Bhatt was born on September 7, 1933 in Ahmedabad, India. She completed her BA from MTB College, Surat in 1952. While in college she volunteered to work on the 1951 census. After her graduation she joined Sir LA Law College in Ahmedabad. In 1954 she received her Law degree and a gold medal for her outstanding work in Hindu Law. Ela R Bhatt is widely recognized as one of the world's most remarkable pioneers and entrepreneurial forces in grassroots development. Known as the "gentle revolutionary" she has dedicated her life to improving the lives of India's poorest and most oppressed women workers, with Gandhian thinking as her source of guidance. In 1972, Ela Bhatt founded the Self-Employed Women's Association [SEWA]–a trade union which has more than 1,000,000 members. Founder Chairperson of the Cooperative Bank of the SEWA, she is also founder and chair of Sa-Dhan [the All India Association of Micro Finance Institutions in India] and founder-chair of the Indian School of Micro-finance for Women. A former Parliament member, Ela R. Bhatt has spent her life fighting for the rights and welfare of India's women workers. She was deeply influenced by Gandhiji, whose ideals she followed all her life. She has been the recipient of honorary doctorates from the SNDT Women's University, the MS University, the Haverford College, USA, the St. Francis Xavier University, Canada and the Harvard University, USA.

Approach of Conflict Transformation

Women's rights movement has contributed to conflict transformation through media development, child protection, project management, humanitarian assistance, human rights protection, human development-health, education, employment and accountability of refugees.

Shirin Ebadi [1947] received the Nobel Peace Prize in 2003 for her efforts for democracy and human rights. She focused her efforts especially on the struggle for the rights of women and children. She is the first Iranian to have been awarded the Nobel Peace Prize. She was awarded the Nobel Peace Prize for her outspoken campaigns for human rights and democracy in her own country of Iran. Shirin Ebadi was born in the city of Hamedan, Iran in 1947. Her family was academics and practicing Muslims. Shirin Ebadi graduated from Tehran University and went onto become Iran's first female judge, serving from 1975. However after the Islamic revolution of 1979 she was forced to resign, as women were no longer allowed to serve as judges. During a long period of unemployment Shirin wrote many books and articles on issues of human rights. In 1992 Shirin finally obtained a lawyer's certificate enabling her to set up her own practice. She defended many victims of child abuse and murder. She has also established two non-governmental organizations in Iran, the Iranian Society for Protecting the Rights of the Child and the Centre for the Defense of Human Rights. Her work for human rights in Iran has won her admiration and respect from humanitarian bodies across the globe. However in Iran her promotion of human rights issues and politically sensitive issues has led to clashes with the conservative judiciary. In 2000 she was given a suspended jail sentence for promoting evidence that prominent conservative leaders were instigating attacks on pro-reform leaders. Besides the Nobel Peace Prize, she has won other awards as well. They are: An official Human Rights

Watch Observer, 1996, the selection of *The Rights of the Child' as Book of the Year by the Culture and Islamic Guidance Ministry and the Rafto Human Rights Foundation prize for human rights activities, Norway 2001.*

There are three stages of Conflict Resolution:

1. Peace building is the process of restoring normal relations between people. It requires the reconciliation of differences, apology and forgiveness of past harm, and the establishment of a cooperative relationship between groups, replacing the adversarial or competitive relationship that used to exist. E.g. the OLAKH, the PUCL and the SAHIYAR [Vadodara, Gujarat];

2. Peacekeeping is the prevention or ending of violence within or between nation-states through the intervention of an outside third party that keeps the warring parties apart. Unlike peacemaking, which involves negotiating a resolution to the issues in conflict, the goal of peacekeeping is simply preventing further violence [The UN Peace Keeping Force, UNHCR in Afghanistan]; and

3. Peacemaking is the term often used to refer to negotiating the resolution of a conflict between people, groups, or nations. It goes beyond peacekeeping to actually deal with the issues in dispute, but falls short of peace building, which aims toward reconciliation and normalization of relations between ordinary people, not just the formal resolution which is written on paper [peace rallies, appeals, and efforts through media].

Women's Contribution in Peace Building

Through sports for peace, quiz for peace, songs for peace, debate/discussion on peace, painting for peace, theatre for peace, politics for peace, rereading history of wars and peace and interfaith dialogues the youth can be motivated towards philosophy of *Vasudhaiv Kutumbakam* [whole world is my family] for Local as well as Global Harmony. The concept of *Vasudhaiv Kutumbakam*- the world is but one family - culture of peace and global citizenship should be inducted into all aspects of human life and education, especially humanities.

Let us celebrate and promote the spirit and philosophy of *Satyam, Shivam, Sundaram* [truth, goodness, and beauty] and live life purposefully and peacefully.

There is a need to create Peace Museums and Peace Galleries to help promote a better understanding of other people and cultures around the world. Organization of peace festivals and peace rallies has become a regular feature in the peace movement. In 2004, over one million people in different part of our globe had candle light marches to stop the US invasion in Iraq.

In this context, for empowering harmony at the individual and community level, liberal humanism needs to be backed by solidarity, service and authority. Educationists like us have:

- To organize and mobilize men, women and children to reiterate and reinforce the importance of secular values for a harmonious coexistence;
- To create pressure groups to condemn acts of violence and

exclusion and to propagate actions and initiatives to promote peace and inclusion;

- To reaffirm secular values and multiculturalism for maintaining and strengthening democratic values based on respect for human rights; and
- To encourage, facilitate and establish similar networks/ coalition of citizens to promote secular values, religious tolerance, democracy and human rights and accelerate women's participation in secular movements striving for equality and justice.

Women's Agency in Peace Keeping

Gandhian women such as Nirmala Deshpande and Medha Patkar have galvanized hundreds of women into peace movement and have brought to the fore women's agency in peace keeping.

Nirmala Deshpande was a noted Gandhian and a Rajya Sabha member. She is best known for her efforts to promote Gandhian ideology, eschew communal violence and usher in peace between India and Pakistan. Popularly known as *Didi* to her followers, 79-year-old Deshpande, clad in white khadi saree, was a familiar figure at functions at institutions connected to the Father of the Nation. Having taken a vow not to get married, Deshpande dedicated her entire life to the promotion of the work and principles of Gandhi and served the deprived and the downtrodden. Her tryst with destiny began in 1952 when she joined the Bhoodan Movement and stayed at Acharya Vinoba Bhave's Paunar Ashram at Wardha near Nagpur. She undertook 40,000 kilometers of padyatras along with Bhave to carry the message of *Gram Swarajya* from state to state. During the historic march, they collected thousands of acres of land donated by those who believed in Gandhiji's ideals and distributed it among poor and landless people. In eighties and nineties, she was the moving spirit behind various peace marches in Punjab and Kashmir. Her peace mission to Kashmir in 1994 and her initiative to organize Indo-Pak meet in 1996 were among major achievements in her decades of public service career. She was conferred the prestigious Rajiv Gandhi National Sadbhavana Award for promoting peace and communal harmony.

The international women's rights movement has decided:

- To organize and mobilize men, women and children to reiterate and reinforce the importance of secular values for a harmonious coexistence;
- To create pressure groups to condemn acts of violence and exclusion and to propagate actions and initiatives to promote peace and inclusion;
- To reaffirm secular values and multiculturalism for maintaining and strengthening democratic values based on respect for human rights;
- To encourage, facilitate and establish similar networks/ coalition of citizens to promote secular values, religious tolerance, democracy and human rights and accelerate women's participation in secular movements striving for equality and justice;
- To counter violence on women, Dalits, minorities, Tribals and to contribute to the efforts for gender justice, social

justice and distributive justice; and

- To consistently raise our voices against fundamentalism and communalism and to initiate action against all forms of discrimination.

Mother Teresa [1910-1997], whose original name was Agnes Gonxha Bojaxhiu, was born on August 26, 1910 in what is now Skopje, Macedonia. On November 29, 1928, at the age of 18, she joined the convent in Ireland and took the name Teresa. The order immediately sent her to India. A few years later, she began teaching at St Mary's High School in Calcutta. She also served there as Principal of the school. In 1948 the Catholic Church granted her permission to leave convent and work among the poor people. In the same year she took Indian citizenship. In 1952 Mother Teresa opened the Nirmal Hriday [pure heart] Home for dying destitutes in Calcutta. She served the people abandoned by society and tried to help and comfort the poor. For over 45 years she helped the poor, sick, orphaned, and dying, while guiding the Missionaries of Charity's expansion, throughout India and then in other countries.

In order to respond better to both the physical and spiritual needs of the poor, Mother Teresa founded the Missionaries of *Charity Brothers* in 1963, in 1976 the contemplative branch of the Sisters, in 1979 the *Contemplative Brothers*, and in 1984 the *Missionaries of Charity Fathers*. Yet her inspiration was not limited to those with religious vocations. She formed the *Co-Workers of Mother Teresa* and the *Sick and Suffering Co-Workers*, people of many faiths and nationalities with which she shared her spirit of prayer, simplicity, sacrifice and her apostolate of humble works of love. Mother Teresa never sought or expected recognition. Yet, she enjoyed universal acclaim as a living saint. In 1979, she won the Nobel Prize in peace for her work with the poor around the world. Her merit and devotion was recognized also by Indian Government and awarded her Padma Shri in 1962 and also the highest honour of the country- Bharat Ratna award on March 22, 1980. Until her death on September 5, 1997, Mother Teresa continued her work among the poorest of the poor.

Like Gandhiji's vision, women's vision of a harmonious society revolve around concerns such as social justice, gender justice and distributive justice. Prospects and possibilities for establishing harmony at the grassroots have increased due to multi-pronged efforts at community level, national and global efforts. Harmony for women's rights movement is:

- Justice, Equality and Peace in the family and the world;
- Harmony at the grassroots is best promoted by those whose stakes are high: the rural poor women from Tribal, Dalit and Minority communities-discriminated thrice over by caste/ethnicity, class and gender; and
- Putting women's concerns in center will ensure development is equitable and sustainable.

Women are adept at bridging ethnic, religious, political, and cultural divides. Under mature leadership they are collaborative, inclined towards consensus and compromise. Experiences of varied memberships in mahila mandals at the village level from different castes, religions, classes come together for common goals.

"For generations, women have served as peace

educators, both in their families and in their societies. They have proved instrumental in building bridges rather than walls."– UN **Secretary-General Kofi Annan**

Women have their fingers on the pulse of the community. They are close to the roots of the conflict, have accurate information about the conflict as information givers/evidence and play a critical role in mobilizing their communities to begin the process of reconciliation and rebuilding once hostilities end. Women are community leaders, with and without formal authority. Both the right and responsibility- drive the peace processes on the ground. Women are often at the center of non-governmental organizations, popular protests, electoral referendums, and other citizen-empowering movements whose influence has grown with the global spread of democracy. Women are highly invested in preventing, stopping, and recovering from conflict, are motivated to protect their children and ensure security for their families. Despite being victims of violence at times of conflict, the consequences of absence of peace are most felt by them. Hence, in all conflict situations, women continue to pursue peace processes as it is expressed in the following pledge taken by women after the Gujarat Riots [2002].

"We, The Women of India, have solemnly resolved to unite our collective wisdom for the betterment of our community and ourselves. We hereby vow to strive towards bringing PEACE and TOGETHERNESS in our families and neighbourhood and work towards communal harmony. To educate ourselves, our men and our children about the values of compassion, love, integrity, honesty,

truthfulness, hard work, acceptance, forgiveness, sharing, respect for humanity and our environment. To raise collective voice against those indulging in suppression, oppression, exploitation, victimization and abuse of ourselves, our men and our children. To strive towards social, economic and political justice, liberty of thought, expression, belief, faith, worship and equality of status and of opportunity for ourselves, our men and our children." –Berndt, Hagen [2006] People building peace, transforming violent conflict in South Asia, Germany: Church Development Service EED.

Bibliography:

- Bhasin, Kamla and Nighat Khan. 2006. *Feminism and its Relevance in South Asia.* Delhi [India]: Kali for Women.
- Bunch, Charlotte. 2002, May. *Feminist Conceptualisation of Peace, Human Rights and Women's Peace Activism.* From proceedings of International Conference in Srilanka on *Women, peace building and Constitution making.*
- Bushra, El. 2003. *Women Building Peace: Sharing Know How.* USA: International Alert, June published by Women's International League for Peace and Freedom.
- International Initiative for Justice. 2003. *Threatened existence: A Feminist Analysis of the Genocide in Gujarat.* Mumbai [India]: New Age Printing Press.
- Kaluagu, Banda Agnes. 2004. *Post Conflict Programmes for Women: Lesions from the Kosovo Women's Initiative.* USA: Gender and Development, Peace Building and Reconstruction, Volume-12, Number 3
- Patel, Vibhuti. 2009. *Fundamentalism, Communalism and Justice,* http://www.europe-solidaire.org/spip.php?article13223

- Skjelsbæk, Inger and Dan Smith. 2001. *Gender, Peace and Conflicty* by International Peace Research Institute. Delhi [India]: Sage Publications.
- Reardon, Betty. 1993. *Women and Peace: Feminist Visions of Global Security*. Delhi [India] Routledge.

Websites:

- www.infochangeindia.org
- www.indiatogether.org
- www.oneworld.net
- www.esocialsciences.com

*****

2
Education Through Communication: An Asian Perspective

Chandrika De Alwis

Abstract: Historical evidence illustrates man's insatiable thirst for domination that drove global conflicts. There was no respect for the way of life practiced by the other, the vanquished. The destruction of the Bamiyaṇ Buddha statues in Afghanistan and the Twin Towers of New York are the modern testimonies to such disregard by man towards man. History also reveals not only military power, but other coercive power methods devised or control mechanisms of powerful nations used against the weaker states. As a result education and development trends of ancient civilizations got lost and buried in the annals of time. The changing nature of power and the futility of armed conflict are well documented in Asian philosophies. The Twenty First Century provides an opportunity to tap into that vast resource of ancient wisdom to propel the educational needs of the global village. The knowledge extracted from these philosophies today is only a drop in the ocean. Asia can lead the way into the lessons of non-violence. This will be an education in itself.

Introduction

Asia has shown the world that development and economic prosperity can be achieved without the use of military might. The shining examples of today are China and India and the Southeast Asian Tiger economies. They impose control mechanisms, but adopted collective bargaining. This is truly remarkable. The collective agreement was the main ingredient in the Asian resurgence rather than competition for power. Another significant factor of the rising economies in the Asian region is that they have not adhered to Western economic models. They found homegrown solutions to suit their individual needs, but at the same time cater to regional cooperation. These educational models are worthy of further investigation for their rich diversity that also reflects adaptability.

Most of these Asian nations, former colonies of the British, French or the Dutch, gained independence from their colonial administrators over sixty years ago. This, so called *Third World Asia*, managed to thwart enormous economic and other pressure mechanisms exerted by the West in their quest for Asian models. The emergences of the East Asian Tiger economies in the late 1980s are good examples. Nevertheless, these nations are still to a certain degree, subject to control systems structured towards Western interests. Such mechanisms could be seen in the form of dependency modules; for economic assistance, cultural affairs and military assistance. [Wriggins, 1970] These controlling efforts are increasingly seen to impound negative effects on the polity, economy and society of the developing countries. The foreign presence or external factors determined and affected the development prospects of the Third World to a large extent observes Wriggins. However, such foreign presence does tend to derive from two parallel and sometimes contradictory considerations is noted by the author. One is the way Asian governments are ready to accept outside support to supplement the terms of their own necessities for political survival. Secondly, in terms of resources needed to deal with problems at the national level, key strategists, the political leaders of these nations, need to consider alternatives to shape their internal policies. The development resurgence in these Asian countries undermines the notion that development is impossible without adherence to Western models or pressure. In addition, the view of the developing world or contemporary representations of the global South are affected by the way the Orient has been historically constructed in Western thinking. [Kabbani, 1986] This is a contributory reason to the continuity of subordination of non-European peoples in Western imagination.

Therefore, in a globalized world today, it is important to ask searching questions about change. [Cheney et al, 2004] Such questions should not be confined to issues of production, employment and efficiency that encompass development, but also about equality, democracy and justice. Huntington [1989] said that we continue to encounter clashes between inconsumerable systems of cultural, religious and social beliefs running cross-grain with the process of globalization. Eurocentric *one dimension of culture and ideology of the modern capitalist world* is profoundly influenced by the dominant Western view. [Amin, 1988: VII] Prevalent even today, these Western driven notions have not been able to curtail the development expansion of the global South.

Academic scrutiny of Asian cultural values in all aspects of social, economic and political endeavors is growing. Even natural science is learning from the region predominantly within traditional medicinal usages and practices. Even the gourmet habits of the Western appetite are turning to Asia for more delectable cuisine. Within this evolving learning curve, this paper draws on the views on the Third World or the global south in comparison to theories that underpin development and modernization in Western thought. Emphasis is laid on how international communication was monopolized by the West to impose a vision that development was not possible in the so called Third or the developing world without adherence to the mechanisms set forth by the West. A closer look at indigenous communication systems and methods facilitates a glimpse into the lessons from the past- to examine education and learning in Asia.

Lessons from the past

In the Song of Reality, a war poem, the stress on words such as freedom, friend, faces, and fighting are a paradoxical mix given an ironical twist to make it economic slander. By interposing the lexicon of business such as counted, balance and sell, the poet identifies the subtleties of economic maneuverings of war. In other words, even war is manipulated for the sake of monetary gain! Brenner [1986] argues that the growth of military expenditure in its present form cannot explain a desire to combat external foes. Instead, it should be perceived as a response to internal economic crises in the Western nations; the military operates at the behest of the growing capitalist class in these countries. Thereby, we see a duality of purpose in conducting war in this present age. This argument may hold true in relation to the present military operations that the UK, the USA, and France are part of... The economic crises they are embroiled in and the emergent capitalist class of Banks in these nations are making headlines is no secret. Today that obsession to dominate the other has taken new meaning as we witness how freedom is transferred to an ideology of us versus them. Theses ideologies are also identified in the Indian epic the *Mahabharata*. ***"War is caused by the clash between right and wrong in order to attain truth and light"***, outlines chapter one of the *Bhagavad-Gita*. The consequences of battle, according to the explanation of Lord Krishna are between evil forces and the good. If the challenge is accepted and won, you will become truly righteous. This is a very philosophical thought, but does not imply to fight the other human you think is evil. The sense of destroying evil outlined in the Gita does not tarnish the victor. Every hero is obliged to wage the Mahabharata war in and through his own life [Commentary on the *Bhagavad-Gita* by Swami Chidbhavananda]. This is the path to self-righteousness, the cardinal principle in the Gita. These thoughts do not ask you to liberate the globe from the throngs of a hateful them.

The question, therefore, is whether we have forgotten to venerate peace and grow with peace? War is cold without any sensitivity to love and security appreciated by ordinary humans. Peace has been hard to come by if we go by the statistics, the sum total of lost human resources. Yet we continue to revere war; we commemorate war to honour the war dead, to remember their ultimate sacrifice in the name of peace. Some examples are the Armistice Day, the Hiroshima and Nagasaki

Day and the ANZAC Day when we offer supreme approval at a holy altar, to pay tribute to the legendary and heroic deeds of the courageous. Yet we forget the irony that all warring factions whether they win or lose believe that they are fighting for justice and freedom. Winston Churchill justified war, even celebrated blood, sweat and tears in his speeches during the Second World War. These are the catch phrases that justify war in a modern sense. These are modern communication spins that aim to propagate an alien ideology from us to them. Such a vision seems to have lost its flavour.

This is where we again turn our attention to the great Indian nation that gave us the global education of non-violence, true freedom and democracy; the many discourse on the topic illustrate that war or armed conflict is futile. Gautama Buddha, the greatest Son of India outlined the *Dasa Raja Dharma* or the Ten Royal Qualities of good governance in the *Cakkavatti Sihananda Sutta.* To be unselfish, to maintain a high moral character, to be prepared to sacrifice for the wellbeing of subjects, to be honest, maintain absolute integrity, to be kind and gentle, lead a simple life for others to emulate, to be free from hatred of any kind exercise non-violence and practice patience; and respect public opinion to promote peace and harmony are these guiding principles.

The Indian role models who emulated these qualities are Emperor Asoka and Mohandas Gandhi. They immortalized the concept of non-violence with their actions more than with their speeches to attain freedom from hunger, freedom from want; both illustrated their wisdom on how to accomplish human dignity without taking to arms. The Battle field of Kalinga changed the outlook of Emperor Asoka completely from a battle hungry emperor to a follower of Gautama Buddha and his teachings to embrace non-violence. As recorded in history, Emperor Asoka is considered to be the one who ruled the Indian Subcontinent. [273 BC to 232 BC] His reign covered almost the whole of India, South Asia; spreading beyond present day Afghanistan to parts of Persia in the west, to Bengal and Assam in the east, and to Mysore in the south. His greatest legacy lives through his achievements in propagating Buddhist principles throughout the world. His practicing *Ahimsa* [non-violence] to spread even as far as ancient Rome and Egypt. He is also accredited as the father of modern diplomacy. [Mendis, 2002] Human rights the *Dharma*, the principles of right life taught by the Buddha, entailed in the UN Charter today were first realized by Asoka. These were paramount ingredients in his monarchy that espoused to treat all his subjects as equals, to give each and every person the path to freedom through tolerance, and equality.

Nonetheless, the way we speak of human rights very broadly at the launch of every conflict today we rarely witnesses the adherence to it. How do we protect human rights through armed conflict? Only the practice of non-violence, as did Asoka and Gandhi, will ensure human rights. Mutual cooperation to attain human goals is the method adopted by ancient civilizations in Asia that prospered and existed for millennia. Though armed conflicts destroyed much of these civilizations Gandhi brought the world attention to the concept of non-cooperation or *Ahimsa* as the means to conquer domination. In Gandhi's words, ***"Non-cooperation is an attempt to awaken the masses to a sense of their dignity and power."*** In that sense both Emperor Asoka and Gandhi placed their fellow human beings at the centre of the philosophy of *Ahimsa*, the principle of refraining from harming any living being. Following closely in the footsteps of Gandhi are the famous Western campaigners such as Martin Luther King of the USA and Nelson Mandela of South Africa, who struggled for their rights to be free from domination and subjugation. They too did not take up arms. As explained by Ravindra Kumar [2009], non-cooperation is the way forward to avoid armed conflict, the tool to battle the disruptive elements that hampers mutual cooperation.

Lessons from the Orient in mutual cooperation, to avoid conflict should be an opening to our troubled conflict ridden world. China and Japan stand out within the region for their history of war and their cmergence to world prominence for many reasons today. These two great countries have much to offer this discourse on knowledge, education and communication. From China comes the Art of War, composed by the ancient Chinese Warrior Sun Tzu. Considered the oldest military treatise in the world and included in the Imperial Chinese Encyclopedia by the year 312 BC war is described as a matter of vital importance to the state, as a matter of life or death, safety or ruination. What is most interesting in these writings are that it also depicts the five direct influences that govern war; the five senses of smell, sound, hearing, taste and touch written in a typical philosophical manner to stress what can be measured, not terms of immeasurability. Thereby, there is no victory as the situations at war are not real challenges; the world knows nothing about them, man wins no reputation for wisdom, nor does he receive credit for courage in overcoming such a trivial matter as a battle. Furthermore, the sun and the moon, the unending rivers are appraised the inexhaustible resources of the earth. Their qualities should be illustrated by great leaders, because if your resources are limitless, there will be victory. Sun Tzu's philosophy, it can be argued, has literally been absorbed by today's China albeit without indulging in military battle. Such, ancient wisdom, knowledge and philosophy seem to be the key elements driving Asian nations like China to restore their former glory. Yet there is no indulgence in armed combat.

Japan too has exemplified to the rest of the world that military might or control is not a necessary ingredient to achieve progress and prosperity. They have accepted humility in their military pursuits. Their philosophy lies in their collective wisdom too to uphold traditional values in bringing back respect, an integral value of Japanese society. They raised Hiroshima and Nagasaki to a level of opulence to erase that horrible memory. They lead the world in technology and their economy is second only to the United States. Also, noteworthy is how Japan spread her wealth without traditional strings of control. Japanese development aid flows freely to the developing nations particularly in the Asian region for training and education. These actions can also be seen as a form of gratitude for making Japan look inwards and correct their errors of judgment. In fact Japan has illustrated their gratitude to Sri Lanka in no uncertain terms because Sri Lanka stood up against the World in 1951 at the San Francisco tribunal to seek that pardon for Japan from the charge of war crimes. A tiny nation like Sri Lanka was able to move the powerful nations to realize that ***"hatred ceaseth not by hatred, but by loving kindness"***, [*Dhammapada*] lessons of loving kindness taught by Gautama

Buddha. Japan invested its energies through loving kindness in every sphere of governance, and economic expansion by transforming their collective values into business corporations to head a revolutionary form of enterprise. However, the very nations that were trying to persecute Japan went back to tactics of power by economic, political or other means. One such example is the controls exerted through the field of international communications particularly on the Third World which gained momentum through the New World Information and Communication Order [NWICO] debate.

The Development Debate

Today an interrelated debate questions whether the term *Third World* is still practical. Owing to the growing diversity of the countries labeled by it and by the changing face of development within the Asian region, it is particularly important to note the emphasis on the usefulness of the very notion of a Third World, notably the feminists, use the term in a subversive way. [Cheney et al, 2004] The second and third worlds an arrogant Western view refers to the rich and ancient cultures and civilizations. Frank [1979] said that it was not precisely accurate to visualize the so called *Third World* as undeveloped [or traditional as modernization theorists would say]. On the other hand, dependency theorists view that under-developed countries exist in a world economic structure decided and dictated by developed capitalist countries. These views are disparate to modernization theory that inquires about internal aspects hampering development. Sklair [1994] built on the dependency approach noting that capitalist structures of the West can offer only a warped form of development to the Third

World. External dynamics actively affected the development prospects of the Third World is no secret and adds an impetus to the views of Wriggins [1970] to believe that within two decades from his writing the West will regret that their inaction. The enormous political problems the governments and peoples of two great countries, India and Pakistan face are contributory note Wriggins; a prophecy certainly true for Pakistan embroiled in a Western led ideological conflict today. However, India has managed to avert such a tragedy through collective action for the benefit of the nation.

Also, the notion of development contained in modernization theory itself becomes problematic in principle. No real alternative to the notion what development underscores is not forthcoming from the West. The debate on development theory has moved into what is known as an *impasse* to identifying some important themes. [Schuurman, 1993] Taking a neo-Weberian view on development Booth [1993], states that *variations in state structure* or *modes of domination* are distinct from societal structures and modes of production [p 53]. This outlook rejects the alternative seen in Marxist and dependency theory wherein politics and culture is thought to be essentially determined by the economy. Booth's perspective focuses on the source of power and greater attention to political structure when compared with Marxism. In developing an *actor oriented* approach Long [1991] criticizes previous development theories for being too deterministic in assuming people's behavior is constrained by societal and international structures. However, Waters [1995] note that the phenomena of globalization as an extension of development need be considered under economic, political and cultural headings.

Amidst all this confusion of analyzing development, Third World nationalist approaches are entirely different. Their view is that successful industrialization and development requires the integration of the Third World into the world economy to adopt a strategy of export oriented industrialization. These views were based on the experiences of newly industrialized countries or the NICs in Latin America and South East Asia. The latter have been at the centre of recent debate because of the economic success they have experienced. The World Bank and IMF frowned on this nationalist approach partly because it sought to gain independence from these entities and partly because of socialist influence on the idea rather than being a capitalist idea. However, Foster-Carter [1985] think that the novelty of the Four Asian Tiger economies and the economic prosperity of Latin American Brazil and Mexico lays not so much in the promotion of their exports but rather in the close involvement of the state in their economic promotion. Harris [1987] consolidates these views saying that these economies were neither free enterprise nor multinational capital that led the process but the deliberate and persistent efforts of governments. In other words, the capitalist business model was substituted by these governments with state involvement that purposefully- encouraged the adaptability of human resources. [Richards, 1993] Thereby these newly growing economies have illustrated their collective responsibility as against the individualistic notions of the Western World. The East Asian experience is described as a success model of free-market capitalism. The model also demonstrates the importance of state involvement in economic planning and development.

Furthermore, nationalism underpins the cultural values of the individual states of the Asian region. Wriggins [1970] wonders whether the powers from the West, the Dutch, French and British influence is written off noting as he observe ***"in fact it is the ethnic elements which are coming back, and have watched this in Ceylon*** [now Sri Lanka]." More and more people are participating in the political process and therefore, begun to assert themselves elaborates Wriggins. ***"They do they do not look at Paris [as in Indo-China] or to Britain as in the case of Colombo; they look to their own tradition, to perceive it and understand it."*** [p.60] Other writers have argued that the promotion of high educational standard initiatives driven by the states in the East Asian NICs, is another important and contributory factor for the socio-economic, socio-cultural and socio-political resurgence of the region. At this point it is relevant to examine how the developing nations made themselves heard and how that process affected the theorizing of culture and communication in the Asian Context.

Information and Communication

Effects of colonization touched all aspects of socio-economic, socio-political and socio-cultural spheres and still resonate in many Asian nations. This scenario provides the backdrop to illustrate the consequences of the dominant positioning of Western global information networks. Technology and communications made it easy for incursions of a capitalist *American way of life* that threatened to undermine traditional cultures, and emphasize consumerism at the expense of community values argued the leaders of the developing world. [Thussu 2000] This phenomenon is particularly evident through the unfair and distorted view of the rest of the world broadcast through international information channels owned and operated by the Western media. The process sparked the New World Information and Communication Order [NWICO] debate in the early 1970s. Leaders from the developing world were vexed that, news processed and sifted by the so called developed countries, broadcast to the rest of the world, and forced a way of projecting the developing countries. [Masmoudi, 1979] The developing nations accused Western media proprietors, their governments and national business communities of gaining from this exercise; the process was seen as responsible for creating a model of dependency that created a negative effect on the polity, economy and society of developing countries. It was seen as a vehicle for communication of US Governments point of view to international audiences. [UNESCO, 1982; Mosco, 1996; Mowlana, 1997] The decisive role of the United States in their ***historical continuities in its quest for systemic power and control of global communication*** was apparent note Schiller. [1998: 23]

Labeled as *free flow* of information, the system served both economic and political purposes that reflected Western, specifically the US loathing of state regulation and censorship of media and its use for propaganda by its communist opponents. [Thussu, 2000] The *free flow* doctrine was complementary to the view that international communication was the key to modernization and development of the so called *Third World*. Even communication research on *modernization* and *development* was based on the belief that mass media would be helpful in transforming traditional societies, another instance of foreign imposition. [Wriggins, 1970] In a comparative survey of five Middle Eastern countries Lerner [1958] found that exposure to media made traditional societies less bound by tradition and to aspire to a new and modern way of life. Modernizers like Lerner failed to comprehend modern versus traditional is not inevitable. For example Islamic traditions continue to define the Muslim world; they have become stronger in the Middle East. [Thussu, 2000]

It can be further argued that the pervasive influence of the West on the traditional societies of the developing world or the former colonies turned these societies inwards, towards their own historical knowledge and traditional culture. To see the perspectives from the field of communication studies is relevant for this analysis. The reasons for these views lie behind the argument that international communication is the vital link that helped monopolize Western viewpoints. Dissanayake [1986] pinpoints two reasons for this; firstly, to widen the field of discourse and facilitate the emergence of new insights from various cultures. Secondly, hypothesizing is more productive and relevant to communication research in non-Western societies rather than to encourage servile adherence to Western communication research credos. Even education was churned out as a commodity in the market place with the growing Western hold on international communication. Also, the American and the Eurocentric communication scholarship attempts to follow more creative pioneers because they do not want to *reinvent the wheel.* [Miike, 2002] Western perspectives are repetitive and lack a clear focus, tackling the problems that seem to be trivial or irrelevant, although methodologically rigorous. [Chu, 1988, page 205] Their reliance on quantitative methodology and statistical analysis sets a limit on investigations further ads Miike. Goonasekera and Kuo [2000] express that ***"the search for an Asian perspective does not imply the outright rejection of Western theories; the issue is the uncritical acceptance of Western models and the neglect of the cumulative wisdom embodied in Asian literature."*** [p. VII] Therefore, it is imperative to examine the rich heritage of Asia, learning through philosophical thought, the historical model of education.

Althusser [1971b] believes that education has now replaced religion as the main state apparatus in the West. Nation states use ideological tools like the media, culture, religion and education to influence the knowledge base. This may be true to a point in the West as their aim is to make national economies competitive within the global economy. By making education and training central components, countries strive to make their economies more productive, efficient and innovative. Marketization of education is now an international phenomenon colonizing the political agenda not only in the UK but also in the US, Canada, New Zealand and Australia. It is daily news that students particularly from the Asian Region are rushing in droves to these countries in pursuit of an educational qualification. The perceptions of a Western academic qualification as better than one in their own lands is yet again achieved by the dominant Western information systems. Wriggins [1970] strongly believed it as important that younger people in the developing countries go to the West for their education but it must not contribute to the brain drain. They ought to return and contribute to their own countries, the skills acquired. This is yet another debatable aspect. However, the region that got labeled as the Third World, can offer the modern world an educational forum that could eventually become the platform for global harmony. The rich heritage of Asia is the hub of a global network of knowledge.

Education and Learning in Asia

The archeological sites of the region reveal the depth of knowledge and the wisdom by which the region governed and maintained their social, political and economic structures. What more remarkable are Asia's indigenous and traditional education systems. They could yield that perfect blend of sustainable education for sustainable development. The hidden engineering and technological feats of bygone civilizations are slowly surfacing somewhat like the Tiger economies. This is in contrast to the idea permeated that only modern technology and Western oriented development approaches work. The world is yet to unearth the hidden treasures of knowledge of these bygone civilizations particularly in Asia. This geographical region is not only confined to Asia but spans the globe from Greece to Japan in a horizontal way and includes the southern tip of South America to Egypt. Situated in present day Pakistan, Takshila, the world's first university was established in 700 BC to pre date Harvard and Oxford. Takshila and Nalanda, the world's first universities, the famous ancient seats of learning in the world are also the finest models. The University of Nalanda situated in Bihar, India is believed to have been built before the Fifth Century AD.

It is the first residential international university of the world. Around two thousand teachers and ten thousand students from all over the Buddhist world lived and studied at Nalanda. Students from China and Korea, Sri Lanka and Indonesia and from all other regions of India studied at Nalanda. Around two thousand teachers and ten thousand students from all over the Buddhist world lived and studied at Nalanda. Learning was greatly encouraged and served dual proposes: knowledge and practice. The subjects taught at Nalanda covered every field of learning including the study of scriptures of Mahayana and Hiinayaana Schools of Buddhism, Brahminical Vedic texts, philosophy, logic theology, grammar, astronomy, mathematics and medicine. More than 10500 students from all over the world studied around sixty subjects here. Among these subjects were the *Vedas* and the eighteen arts or skills that include archery, hunting and elephant lore. In addition the University had a school of law, school of medicine and a school for military science. The famous treatise known as *Arthashastra* or the knowledge of economics was composed here by Chanakya. The legendary scholars from Takshila are the Maurya Emperor Chandragupta and Charaka, the Ayurveda healer. Its importance as a monastic university continued until the end of the Twelfth Century AD. Descriptions of Takshila were written in Sri Lanka in the Fifth Century AD.

Histories, religions, and philosophies in Asia are *rich storehouses* for conceptualizing Asiacentric models of communication contexts [Ishii, 1998] and Chen, 1998. In this day it is worthwhile to take note of the Buddhist philosophy that nothing is permanent which exemplifies today's changing world not only in inventions but also the evolving environmental scenario. Sharp differences in cultural traditions certainly exist throughout Asia. Multiple strands have evolved over time due to various religious, philosophical, political, economic, and geographical factors. [Jensen, 1992] and Dissanayake [1983] observes, ***"What is important in human communication is to find out how a receiver makes sense of verbal stimuli received and engages in a search for meaning. And this search is an inward one."*** [page 29] This is the Indian indigenous model. Asia's indigenous and traditional education systems could yield that perfect blend of sustainable education for sustainable development is therefore a prudent argument.

Also, the theories of language are taking an increasing role in social thinking in recent years for two reasons. First it looks at language as inherently social. Secondly language attempts to analyze our existence in society. The link between these two is said to be human consciousness. The implication is that humans could gain knowledge of the outside world through rational thinking. Communication is central to understanding and agreement. Habermas [1981] was also concerned with language, ideas and symbols and the role they can play in the struggle for cooperation. Today the need enhance cooperation rather than domination is certainly possible through advanced communication and information technologies. There is every possibility to utilize these resources for a new educational information order. This is the point of departure from conflict to cooperation: Thereby the need for domination of one model over the other will cease to make way for cooperative engagement.

Bibliography:

- Althusser, L. 1971. *Ideology and ideological state apparatus* in L. Althusser's Lenin and Philosophy and Other Essays. London [UK]: New Left Books.

- Amin, S. 1988. *Eurocentrism. Translated by R. Moore.* New York [USA]: Monthly Review Press.
- Booth, D. 1993. Development Research: From Impasse to a New Agenda in FJ Schuurman [ed.] *Beyond the Impasse: New Directions in Development Theory.* London [UK], Zed.
- Brenner, R. 1986. *The Social Bias of Economic Development* in J Roemer [ed.] *Analytical Marxism.* Cambridge [UK]: Cambridge University Press.
- Chen, GM. 1998. *A Chinese Model of Human Relationship Development* in BL Hoffer and JH Hoo [eds.] *Cross-Cultural Communication East and West in the Nineties,* pp. 45-53. San Antonia, TX [USA]: Institute for Cross-Cultural Research of Trinity University.
- Cheney, G, Christensen, LT, Zorn, TE and Ganesh S. 2004. *Organizational Communication in an Age of Globalization: Issues, Reflections, Practices. Prospect Heights.* Illinois [USA]: Waveland Press Inc.
- Chu, GC. 1988. *In Search of an Asian Perspective of Communication Theory* in W Dissanayake, [ed.] *Communication Theory: The Asian Perspective,* pp. 204-210. Singapore [USA]: Asian Mass Communication Research and Information Centre.
- Dissanayake, W [1986]. *The Need for the Study of Asian Approaches to Communication,* pp. 6-13 Media Asia, 13 [1].
- Dissanayake, W. 1983. *The Communication Significance of the Buddhist Concept of Dependent Co-origination, Communication,* 8 [1], pp. 29-45
- Foster-Carter, A [ed.]. 1985. *The sociology of development'. In M Haralambos Sociology: New Directions.* Ormskirk: Causeway Press.
- Frank, AG. 1979. *Dependent Accumulation and Under-development.* New York: Monthly Review Press.

- Goonasekera, A and Kuo, ECY. 2000. *Forward-Toward an Asian Theory of Communication?* Asian Journal of Communication, 10 [2], vii-xii
- Habermas, J. 1981. *Theory of Communicative Action*, London [UK]: Heinemann.
- Harris, N. 1987. *The End of the Third World.* Harmondsworth: Penguin.
- Huntington, SP. 1989. *The Errors of Endism.* The National Interest, 3-16
- Ishii, S. 1998. *Developing a Buddhist En-Based Systems Paradigm for the Study of Japanese Human Relationships.* Japan Review-10, 109-122
- Jensen, JV. 1992. *Values and practices in Asian Argumentation.* Argumentation and Advocacy 28 [4], 153-166
- Kabbani, R. 1986. *Europe's Myths of Orient.* London [UK]: Pandora Press.
- Kumar, Ravindra. 2009. *Non-Cooperation.* Meerut [India]: World Peace Movement Trust.
- Lerner, D. 1958. *The passing of Traditional Society: Modernizing the Middle East.* New York [USA]: Free Press.
- Long, N. 1991. *Heterogeneity, Actor and Structure: Towards a Reconstitution of the Concept of Structure.* Unpublished paper quoted in Booth in 1993
- Masmoudi, M. 1979. *The New World Information Order.* Journal of Communication, 29 [2], pp.172-85
- Miike, Y. 2002. *Theorizing Culture and Communication in the Asian Context: An Assumptive Foundation.* Intercultural Communication Studies, XI [1]:1-21
- Osco, V. 1996. *The Political Economy of Communication: Rethinking and Renewal.* London [UK]: Sage.

- Mowlana, H. 1997. *Global Information and World Communication: New Frontiers in International Relations* [Second Edition]. London [UK]: Sage.
- Richards, A. 1993. *Korea, Taiwan, and Thailand: Trade Liberalization and Economic Growth* in October Issue of OECD Observer.
- Schuurman, FJ. [ed]. 1993. *Beyond the Impasse: New Directions in Development Theory.* London [UK], Zed.
- Schiller, H. 1998. *Striving for Communication Dominance: A Half-Century Review* in D Thussu [ed.] *Electronic Empires.* London [UK]: Arnold.
- Sklair, L. [ed]. 1994. *Capitalism and Development.* London [UK]: Rutledge.
- Thussu, DK. 2000. *International Communication: Continuity and Change*: Hodder: Arnold Publication.
- UNESCO. 1982. *Culture Industries: A Challenge for the Future of Culture.* Paris [France]: United Nations Economic, Social and Cultural Organization.
- Waters, M. 1995. *Globalization.* London [UK]: Rutledge.
- Wriggins, Howard. 1970. *The Presence in Southern Asia of outside Powers.* Annals of the American Academy of Political Science 390:48-62

*****

3

Education of Heart: An Essential Foundation for Peace

Patricia Hess

Abstract: The goals of our education institutions and the goal of peace are not aligned; in fact, a trend of divergence can be seen by the increase in violence, crime, and immorality among students. Education during youth is a foundation for social interactions throughout life - thus, it has the power to turn people towards peace or conflict. Western societies have promoted formal schooling as a social standard for the world to follow; however, the paradigm for modern education was established at a time when advanced media technologies, such as video and the internet, were not available. This paper seeks to clarify whether the original paradigm of teaching students in classrooms that are segregated by age groups is still necessary, and how this system of education has affected social development. Secondly, an alternative system of education is discussed with a focus on the practical goals of education and ways for people in poverty to gain access to high levels of educational achievement without the burdens of expensive institutions. Finally, education is looked at as a social tool for peace, from the perspective that it can be used to promote values of morality and heart. An essential point here is the need for a deep connectedness of young people with their families and communities, in relationships where character is strongly influenced; this vital social development is limited by the current system of education because of the time students spend separated into peer groups. Conclusively, a new system of education could easily be designed based on media technologies and small support groups, and it would provide the opportunity for self-paced, self-motivated learning as well as making educational achievement more accessible to the poor. In addition, it could greatly contribute to the cause of peace by rejuvenating family values.

Introduction

In considering what influences youth to become people, who contribute to peace, rather than people who cause conflict or commit crimes, it is essential to evaluate the social dynamics that shape their hearts - their capacity to love, to have good ethics, and to show concern for others. In countries where school attendance is compulsory, schools are the most significantly influential social environment that shape young hearts. Unfortunately, though, in America, as well as other nations, there is a downward trend in the quality of character among school students. This is evidenced by the rash of school violence and problems associated with crime and immorality that have often been seen in the news.

Therefore, it is vitally important to re-evaluate the traditional education system from a sociological perspective. These are some of the questions that could be asked:

1. How do the social groups of the classroom and school affect individual students?
2. How do the social groups of schools affect families and communities?
3. How does the school environment contribute to the downward trend of students' ethics and morals? and
4. How could the education system be changed in a way that would affect the development of students' characters?

Qualities of heart begin forming in early childhood and often become concrete by young adulthood. That means the school years are the most important period for developing character, and, thus, the main factor that will decide whether a person lives an altruistic life in harmony with others or a self-centered life in conflict with others. A significant part of that formative process is a child's own motivation and will, but even how youth challenge themselves is tied in with their school experiences. One of the most destructive forces upon our future generations is the loss of motivation to learn. When an educational environment degrades to the point that students give up making effort, then that education system should be dismantled and a new system should be made that will stimulate students to challenge themselves and actively work toward their educational goals.

Part 1: Is it time for a new paradigm?

At the beginning of the history of education, the system of a teacher lecturing to a classroom of students was the most efficient method of learning. Of course, back then, they did not have advanced media technologies, and published information was limited. For example, if a teacher's personal research was included in the course, then the individual teacher was likely the only source from which to obtain it. With teachers as the main source of information, rather than media, then it was necessary for the students to come to the teacher.

From there, institutions sprang up as a venue for students' access to teachers. However, the social culture that has developed in schools and colleges has become antithetical to the goal of education. For example, in America, some students might have the ability to make high grades but will purposely make average grades because they might be persecuted by their peers. In a group, the majority make average grades, and the majority controls the social atmosphere, so the 'socially correct' behavior of the group will be to make average grades - those who don't will be outside of the norm and, therefore, at risk of ostracism.

This same phenomenon happens with the morality of the group. When students from different family backgrounds are put together, those with high ethical standards are in the minority, so they tend to compromise their own values to adopt those of the group majority. When this takes place generation after generation, the 'average' that defines the majority gets lower and lower.

Also, with the onset of media technology over the past century, the effect of this group dynamic has been multiplied. Through media, companies compete to appeal to the most people possible, so they target the majority, or the *average* person. Therefore, because the *average* behaviour in the classroom is echoed through the media, the students in the minority are even more pressured to conform.

Social conformity among youth has contributed to the current situation of education and has affected society as a whole. In developed countries that provide free, compulsory primary education and reasonably easy access to higher education, there are severe problems with student apathy and moral behavior. Students who grow up in an educational system that indirectly perpetuates sexual immorality and substance abuse become the next generation of citizens and pull down the level of the nation's social integrity. Despite schools providing education directly against sex, drugs and alcohol, they have not been able to control the group social dynamics that will naturally occur in any institutional setting where the ratio of adults to students and the effectiveness of adult supervision are small.

Another effect of institutionalizing education has been the need to establish requirements for diplomas or degrees. This also contributes to student apathy when courses are not useful for life goals [such as employment] and if the courses have content that is repetitive. For example, from primary school through college, students may have to take five or more national history classes –although each class may provide more detail than the previous one, the same basic information is repeated. Students sometimes continue to submit the same reports with only a few facts added. The repetition is boring for both students and teachers, and it wastes a great deal of educational resources, including staff time, use of facilities and curriculum materials.

Inefficiency is compounded by the expense of education, which burdens students and their parents, and even the whole society, in the case of America and other nations that have government funded public schools and college subsidies. Since most college textbooks, including the curricula used by famous universities can be purchased for a small fraction of the cost of tuition, then the price is not for the information - it's a money game about obtaining a high social status and getting a well-paid job.

The greatest waste is from falsely inflated college tuition, housing and meal services. When colleges require first and second year students to live on campus, they are keeping a monopolized micro-economy in place. And, when the tuition of famous universities are five to ten times higher than the lowest priced schools, then the expense is less about educational quality and more about taking advantage of the economic principle of *supply and demand* in regard to admissions.

Notice the self-feeding loop: only wealthy people can afford the schools on the high-end of the tuition scale, so those who already have high social status add to the reputation of the university while they are students and again, later, when they get good jobs through their circle of wealthy friends and relatives. That is, once a university is able to attract wealthy students, educational quality does not need to be the deciding factor for tuition rates. The *supply* of sought-after universities will always remain low as a natural result of social behavior: Given a choice of many boxes in different sizes and styles, everyone will choose the box with the most money in it.

Money makes it difficult for students to get into schools, but that's not all - money makes it impossible for education to be only about learning. Students who are taking a required course of study for a diploma or degree are usually doing so for one main purpose: to get a good job. Therefore, their focus of interest is not purely on learning for the excitement of knowing new things; their mind-set is on finishing the requirements as quickly and easily as possible so they can obtain the end result. That's not so much of a problem unless students know they won't be able to get good jobs. If their society is such that job prospects are not hopeful, no matter how well they do in school, then they lose their motivation to make effort in their studies. This is especially a problem of high school students in compulsory public education programs when they are required to be in the classroom but have no interest in learning.

The flip-side of society's effect on education is the effect of schools on their social environment. It has been commonly thought that removing children from their family for the majority of their waking hours and separating them by age groups is somehow better for the children. This is only a myth left over from the Western European culture that made it socially correct for wealthy people to send their kids to boarding schools. Others that have wanted to look rich and cultured have mimicked that practice; for example, in Korean schools, students are dressed in the British style of school uniforms, and they stay at school as much as possible - with some public schools encouraging boarding, even when families live nearby and it's not necessary.

The side-effect of this practice is a major reduction in the amount of time children have to interact with their parents, siblings, other relatives, and people in the community. Therefore, it should not be assumed that the institutional style of education is the best option. In traditional tribal and agricultural lifestyles, children were important contributors to the stability and cohesiveness of families and social groups. They cared for younger siblings and did work to help provide for their family's needs; in so doing, they developed their abilities and skills, sense of responsibility, bonds of heart, and the capacity to relate to others of different ages and generations.

Many of the qualities of character and interpersonal relationships that naturally developed from those lifestyles have diminished because of the amount of time students are separated from their families. Over time, families and communities adapted to children being in school; now, in countries with industrialized economies, often both parents work - so they depend on schools to raise their children, but when the schools fail to instill values, their communities are troubled by juvenile delinquency.

Society as a whole has been negatively affected by the system of education in institutions, and social pressures often prevent students from achieving the benefits of education that would be expected from the amount of time and they spend for school. When students are not motivated to learn, but are required to be in classrooms [either by compulsory attendance laws or social norms], the situation creates a group mind-set similar to that of people in prison. Not only do their thoughts wander far outside the classroom walls, but, also, their hearts develop resentment, which can affect their behavior and emotional development - in turn, that echoes to family and community relationships.

This situation is especially true in South Korea, where high school students often stay at public schools or go to private academies to study until 10 pm at night; extra time is put in on Saturdays and during vacation times as well. In fact, a Korean student, whom I personally know, described his experience as *like being in prison* because he had to stay at school, but the social atmosphere was not conducive to studying and there was nothing else to do. Despite all the hours and money invested, few public school students attain the academic level required for entrance to the main Korean universities, and Korean employers have indicated that, generally, graduates are not well prepared for the workforce.

There are specific factors that contribute to the 'wheel-spinning' effect of education in South Korea - caused by a mix of policy, culture and student motivation. For example, it is a standard practice to use a *curve* in grading that limits the number of 'A's' [grades of 90/100], and students are ranked within their classes, so there is only room for one student in each place [first, second, third, etc.]. If a student's grade or rank falls, his or her parents storm into the school and yell at the teacher; they are viciously competitive, and instances of bribery and cheating are often in the news. [This is because only the top students have a chance to go to the famous universities, and education is a major determinant of social status.]

Furthermore, if a whole class makes low grades, the teacher is blamed for either not teaching effectively or making the test too hard. And, regardless of students' grades, they pass and get their diplomas. Therefore, students know they can get through school without really making effort, and they also know that - even if they make a lot of effort - there is no room at the top of the class. The biggest effort is made by parents, who spend a fortune on private education to keep up the hope, or at least the appearance, that their children are headed for the most esteemed university.

When the culture is such that the social pressure is on the teachers and school administrators to give students passing grades and allow them to graduate, then rigid standards of educational quality cannot be held in place. Schools are forced to accommodate both the demands of parents and the requirements of governing organizations that provide funding. With teachers adapting their tests to the level of students and schools adopting graduation policies that keep their statistics level, the lowering of educational standards over time is hidden.

The change in standards, however, is obvious to those who are old enough to remember the way schools used to be. I once had an elderly American college teacher express to me her shock and frustration over apathetic students who did not study or complete their assignments; in the forty or so years since she had attended college, the standards of students' motivation and effort - as well as the course requirements - had drastically declined. Returning to the standards of schools several generations ago would not be an answer to the problem and may not even be possible, given the changes that have occurred in social attitudes. The authoritarian atmosphere of schools could only be supported by strong family unity and discipline in homes.

Taking all this into account, it is clear that a new paradigm for an educational system is needed for the sake of maintaining and improving the social integrity of future generations. It is needed for the sake of liberating students to reach their full potential. And, it is needed for the sake of the poor in nations that don't have resources for building and maintaining institutions.

Underdeveloped nations have often copied the examples of wealthy western nations with the hopes that duplicating their social systems will bring them the same kind of success. They have tended to overlook the fact that the economies of the leading countries flourish only because they can take advantage of comparatively cheap resources and labor from the poor countries. Thus, they should carefully scrutinize the results of western education practices before making decisions about the future of their own education systems.

Part 2: A Plan for Self-Motivated Learning

Now that people are awash in information from the internet, and don't need to be contained inside a classroom to obtain it, how can they gain recognition for their learning without going to an educational institution? Though online learning has become widely available, and is even offered by prestigious traditional universities, many people are not confident that degrees obtained from online studies have the same status and quality as traditional degrees. This is partly because of fake schools that sell degrees without providing genuine instruction, but it is also because there are no universal standards for evaluating independently attained knowledge.

That considered, the first essential point of a new paradigm for education would be to create a globally consistent testing system. And, to deal with historical inequalities from access to education, a testing system should be designed in the spirit of charity - to keep it as free and accessible as possible, while, at the same time, ensuring it will develop a reputation of quality and genuineness [independent of profit motives].

A way to do that would be for an international non-profit organization, such as the UNESCO, to formulate and oversee a system of evaluation and ensure that fees for testing were not monopolized by profit making entities. Standard fees could be adopted based on the prices and wages of each country, and fee waivers could be offered for the poor, balanced by higher charges for the rich. One of the main benefits of a new testing system would be to provide opportunities for the poor to achieve recognition for their studies without having to pay the price of the land, buildings, and staff, etc., that are necessary for traditional education.

Making tests universally accessible might mean they wouldn't be sought after, because people seek social status from exclusive schools. But, making the tests more difficult and extensive than regular tests could counteract that effect and give credibility to the system. That is to say, if passing was too easy, it would be thought of as a low level of education, but if it was difficult, it would be seen as a prestigious accomplishment.

Precautions must be taken in order for a reputation of trust and value to be built around a new testing system because there will always be those who try to cheat. For example, there is sometimes the question of whether the student named on the test is actually the person who took the test. This could be solved by a combination of identification by video and fingerprinting. And, since most problems of this type happen because one or more people in a supervisory position allow it to, then there could be a secondary type of monitoring that is not accessible by those who are in direct contact with the test takers, and grading could also be done by a neutral staff or by computer.

There would also be problems to solve in designing evaluations with the capacity to measure the same skills that students demonstrate in classrooms. Course work such as reports or presentations would need to be adapted to test formats, since information and communication over the internet makes it too easy for students to plagiarize or substitute the work of others as their own. There would need to be a way for students to be observed while they are producing materials equivalent to course work.

Therefore, tests should be developed for different skill types, such as the following:

A. Comprehension and memorization of information;
B. Synthesizing facts in written form, as in essays or reports;
C. Verbal and visual presentations of ideas, as in business plans or slide shows;
D. Analyzing theories or functions, as in scientific studies or technological developments; and

E. Applied skills, as in mathematics or vocational subjects.

Other skill types may be added as needed for specific subjects, and not all subjects would require testing for each skill type. That would give flexibility for students to focus on the purpose of their education; for example, someone wanting to be an engineer would take skill type tests D and E, while someone planning to go into sales would take tests B and C.

In traditional schools, there has been the problem of students bypassing genuine learning because they are studying only the content of the tests or unfairly obtaining test answers. To negate that, *skill type A* could be an entirely straightforward testing method with write-in answers [rather than multiple choices that encourage guessing]. All questions for the test would be provided as study material, exactly as they would appear on the test. At the time of testing, a computer program would choose a random selection of questions from the study list, so that each student would have a different mix of questions. [In places without computers, tests could be printed and sent from another site.]

To be evaluated for *genuine learning*, rather than the memorization of facts, students would need to take skill type B, C, D, or E tests, designed so they must demonstrate skills at the testing site, rather than turning in previously completed works. Such tests could be done in a number of sessions, and students could use on-site materials or an intranet database to complete essays, reports, or presentations. Advanced studies, such as experiments to confirm hypotheses, would require extended supervision to verify their authenticity, and special facilities may be needed, such as science or technology labs;

these could be accessed through current research institutions. Likewise, vocational testing could be done in cooperation with places of employment.

In addition to skill types, students could be evaluated by knowledge levels. This would substitute for grade levels, and it would stimulate self-paced learning while eliminating the repetition of similar course information in different grades. After passing a knowledge level, students would not need to be tested on the same information again. For example, the Hundred Most important facts of history might be *knowledge level-1*, but *knowledge level-2* would not cover the same facts; it would be additional details or new information. For convenience in transferring to and from traditional schools, the levels and skills that are tested could be categorized in comparison to traditional grade levels, but there should not be age requirements or limits for taking the tests. To incorporate principles of self-motivated learning, students should be free to advance to any level or skill at any age.

Therefore, there would be more than one dimension to testing - students would advance in a vertical way through knowledge levels [how much information is learned] and in a horizontal way through skill types [how information is applied]. Depth could be added as a third dimension through evaluating creativity [original ideas based on learned information].

To deal with compulsory education laws, instead of the deciding factor being the age of the students, it could be a certain level of tests. Ideally, any legal requirements for school attendance should be limited to students who are in the process of training to study independently -that is, they are acquiring basic reading, writing, math and study skills. Once they can establish, through evaluations, that they have the capacity to study on their own, and then compulsory attendance should be waived. Though there may be both good and bad repercussions of this, any debate would be canceled by the fact that it would be impractical and nearly impossible to monitor a large number of independent students.

It is commonly thought that if children are in thc school all day, then they won't be subjected to child labor or get into gangs, which are problems in some areas. However, regulating school attendance doesn't eliminate those problems, and creates others, as mentioned in Part-1. There could be a separate social agency to deal with issues of child abuse or delinquency. Also, the concept that children shouldn't work at all is contrary to traditional agricultural and tribal lifestyles. Contributing to the work done by their family and community is a way for children to learn life skills and a sense of responsibility.

Compulsory attendance would impede self-paced, self-motivated learning because students would not be inspired to challenge themselves unless they could finish school more quickly. An assumption is made that if students are in schools, they are learning - but that is not always true. Whether being taught in a classroom or studying independently, a student can either do the minimum or invest to the maximum. In addition, much of teachers' time is spent managing classes and repeating information from the text; the amount of actual teaching is a smaller percentage of the class time.

Think about it: if all the information for a diploma is online [or in library books] and available for free, why should students and taxpayers have to pay tuition? In this new paradigm, after basic skills are attained [such as in grades 1-3], the price of an education should be only for the actual testing costs. Tutoring or class instruction could be organized independently by parents or the community, as needed, and funded separately; also, the direct involvement of parents in the selection of teachers would negate the need for government regulations and licensing, further reducing taxpayer burdens.

Although designing extensive and specific evaluations would cost more than traditional testing methods, it would still be much less than the expense of keeping students inside classrooms for the greater part of sixteen or more years. The main bonus would be that this new paradigm for test-based diplomas and degrees could stimulate self-motivated learning so students would challenge themselves and invest their whole hearts and minds into achieving their future goals.

The following is an outline of the main points of a test-based education:

1. Diplomas and degrees would be awarded based on a new method of testing that would not require enrollment in a course or school; there would be reasonable fees for testing, but there would not be tuition fees. For:

A. Testing formats and fees would be established by a non-profit, global organization, such as the UNESCO, to keep standards consistent worldwide and to ensure the tests remained accessible to the poor;

B. Tests would be more complex and extensive in order to assess students' capacities for completing papers, projects, research, or other skills that have been demonstrated in traditional courses;

C. Questions for tests based only on memorization of facts would be freely provided as study material to avoid problems of unfair access to test questions; other types of tests would be used to assess applications of knowledge, such as essays, reports, lab or vocational skills, and problem solving; and

D. Verification of students' identities, monitoring during tests, and grading tests would be overseen by third parties via video and internet, in order to prevent false records and maintain a reputation of integrity.

2. Formats for education should be flexible and adaptive for different learning abilities, various needs, and diverse localities. For:

A. Most students would study independently after being trained in self-motivated learning techniques; they could use any source of information rather than a certain curricula;

B. Students who are unable or unwilling to study independently could enroll in traditional courses to study either online or in classrooms with teachers; there would be no government regulations for teachers, the parents, communities or schools who employed them would determine requirements;

C. There would be no age requirements for passing through higher levels of education; students could progress as slowly or quickly as they wanted to, for the purpose of stimulating self-motivated learning; and

D. Compulsory education laws would be limited to verifying that students have achieved a level of education sufficient to study independently and are allowed the opportunity to do so, and would not dictate specific days, hours, or curriculum for study.

Part 3: Education of the Heart

From the perspective of Rev. Dr. Sun Myung Moon, the purpose of human life is not intellectual achievement; the true purpose is to develop and practice the ability to love others. However, so much emphasis has been put on a secular system of education that essential values and ethics based on altruism and brotherly love have been bypassed. Plus, being confined to peer groups with large student-to-teacher ratios has limited the potential for learning through relationships. An education system designed for self-motivated and individually-paced learning in small groups of mixed ages, that would offer ample time for social interactions with parents and mentors, would be an ideal learning environment for *education of the heart*.

Intellectualism has a temporal value related to economic and social standing, whereas heart has an eternal value. Even from a secular perspective, heart has the value of creating social harmony. Although education has an immediate goal of preparing students to be functional in socio-economic positions, it is even more important to use the learning environment to prepare students to be citizens who contribute to the welfare and peace of their nation and world. While the percent of people, who have received formal schooling in developed nations has greatly increased over the past century, so also have the social problems related to a lack of caring and concern for others - signs of an absence of heart. There may be many factors contributing to this, but, certainly, something is awry with the education system. In America, schools are rampant with immorality and continue to spawn suicidal shooting sprees. Instead of rising up young people who will benefit society, schools may end up producing youth who get involved in crime and conflict.

The kind of learning environment children grow up with, molded by the purposes of the education system, will affect the potential for them to be people of peace or conflict. Character is primarily shaped during the time of infancy through young adulthood - the time of attending schools. Once attitudes and heart are established, it is very difficult to change them. There is always the hope that the next generation of leaders will be able to solve the problems of the world, but will they be any different, having been raised in the same kind of learning environment [or worse]?

True social change doesn't come from forced revolutions and political takeovers. Such actions are only effective until those with a stronger army or more votes push them out again. Lasting peace must grow from the roots of society: it's children. It must come to blossom within their hearts. The values and lifestyle that will bring about social harmony must be honored, modeled and actively taught. Even though the ideal is simple, the difficulty of its application is multiplied by every sub-culture, ethnic group and community when they can't agree on which ethics is correct.

Watering down' ethics to bring a consensus won't work; that's already been tried. First and foremost, it must be admitted that secularism has failed to bring peace. In fact, it is responsible for inducing Jihad. Secularism might as well be pronounced, *sexualism* because of the widespread tolerance and outright support for homosexuality, pre-marital sex, infidelity, promiscuity, pornography, and even prostitution that has infected the world, primarily through the American culture. If the many religions of America had cooperated to establish a society with sexual morality, there would have been no fury to fuel Islamic attacks.

Secularism was embraced by the public school system in America as a way to suppress religious recruitment and create a *neutral ground*-a non-religious learning environment. Support for secularism flowed from the following sources:

1. Schools of psychology put out the idea that there is no Creator and no spiritual dimension other than thought;
2. Schools of science introduced 'proof' that everything evolved by its own will, without Divine intervention; and
3. Schools of government and history continually pointed to religions as sources of conflict and oppression - translating the constitutional *freedom of religion* into a *freedom from religion.*

The result has been that *freedom*, in and of itself, without a religious context, became the main ideal promoted by secular education. While there have been some positive outcomes of the freedom ideal [such as reduced racism and racially integrated schools], the defense of sexual immorality in the name of *freedom* has degraded the society to a sub-human level - where sex is as low or lower than the behavior of animals. Hand in hand with that trend has been the 'freedom' of people doing anything they want in privacy - such as using illegal drugs. Just fifty years ago, community streets were safe places for children to play, but after the idolization of individual freedoms at the sacrifice of family values, parents have to live in fear that their children will be victims of drug gangs, pimps, or rapists.

The kind of heart needed for a peaceful, crime free society is altruistic heart - and that is not acquired in an atmosphere of selfish individualism. Reverend Moon teaches that families can be schools of love when the relationships within them are altruistic: People who have learned to love their parents, spouse, siblings, and children more than themselves will be people who can lead the world into peace. Yet, when families are already broken by sexual immorality, or mired in substance abuse, there is little hope for children to adopt such heart.

In that sense, there is a great need for a learning environment to fill the vacancies of dysfunctional families. Thus, social groups modeled after extended families would be best. As mentioned previously, small groups that would offer abundant adult-child interaction, with students and mentors of varied ages to facilitate intergenerational bonds, would be the kind of social structure that could convey values and instill altruistic heart.

It is possible for students to study independently using a computer or books; however, if children are unsupervised in their free time, they will usually play games instead of studying. Therefore, even though curricula and teachers could be available online, there might still be a need for a supervised study group. It would be most important to have small groups with adults who relate closely with the students, who know them both in and out of the educational setting, and who are in a position to both mentor and discipline them.

Parents would be best, but few have the time and situation to be able to home-school, and it is sometimes difficult to relate to children from the dual roles of parent and teacher. In America, many families have turned to homeschooling, but that is not possible if both parents are working or if parents lack the ability to teach or discipline their children. And, although the family atmosphere should be the ideal choice for moral support, there are sometimes problems of immorality within families.

Adults who supervise study groups would not need to be tutors or teachers because educators could be accessed online. That could be a better situation for teachers, as well; just as it is difficult for a single parent to play the roles of both nurturer and disciplinarian, it is also hard for teachers to focus on controlling students' behavior at the same time as teaching them, especially if their relationship does not extend beyond the classroom. Also, a more efficient use of professional teachers' time and skills would be in an interactive online classroom; the best teachers could have an unlimited number of students.

An option that could provide a similar social support structure as a family wouid be small groups of ten to fifteen students supervised by at least two adults. It would be best to have various ages of students in a group, rather than same-aged peers, so it would be more like a family with older and younger siblings. That way, students would be motivated to help the younger ones, rather than trying to do the same things as their peers.

Changing the current American education system from the *inside out* would be an endless battle, because its secularism and freedoms have already been defended by courts. Change will have to come from the 'outside in' - and it has already begun through the home-schooling movement, which has advanced the right of parents to keep their children out of schools. The wave of *freedom of secularism* can, ironically, be used to propel *freedom from secularism.*

Three factors are essential for lifting our future generations out of secularism:

1. Unity of various religious and moral groups on the sexual and social ethics that will support the stability of families and the development of altruistic heart;
2. Political and social action to establish an education system that can transmit those ethics in a learning environment similar to a loving, extended family; and
3. Motivational factors that will encourage students to voluntarily participate, such as self-paced learning, minimal fees, and degrees that open economic and social opportunities.

To design an educational system that will produce graduates who can contribute to peace, the main focus should be the development of heart. However, world history is full of examples of strong governments and religions that could not succeed in forcing their ethics upon people. The problem is that love can't be forced or dictated; no one can command someone to be altruistic. Ethics have to come from inside each person's heart. Therefore, laws and regulations might pave the way for education of the heart, but enforcement is not the way to accomplish it.

The desire to achieve something is increased by the perceived benefits, which generally amount to some form of social approval. For example, students might dream of being famous singers because they imagine everyone would cheer for them and admire their riches. Likewise, the energy that gives students the impetus to start and complete a course of study is the anticipation of socio-economic rewards. Therefore, creating a system of social approval that rewards students for their ethics would be more significant than any curricula or teaching method. When young people start competing to be the most altruistic, then the learning environment that guided them to that place of heart will have been a success.

Conclusion

In re-evaluating education, the following steps should be considered:

1. What is the intended purpose of the current education system, and is that aligned with its functional purpose? [For example, the intended purpose of a liberal arts degree is to gain a broad understanding of society and history, but the functional purpose may be to get a job in which liberal arts knowledge is not used.];
2. What kind of learning environment is there, and will it

contribute to the quality of students' characters in such a way that they become people who will bring peace to the world? and

3. What opportunities for achievement and social approval are there, and are they great enough to stimulate voluntary, self-motivated participation and advancement?

Overall, the basic idea of education should be changed from the perspective of passively being taught to the perspective of actively taking initiative to learn. Rather than repeating information from a text, teachers should be teaching students how to learn on their own - how to study, how to use information, and how to practice and memorize. The amount of time, money and resources that could be saved by this simple change in the approach to learning would be astronomical. For nations that haven't already invested heavily in the traditional model of schooling, this plan for self-paced, self-motivated learning is a viable option that would be more flexible, efficient and economical.

Finally, all the parts of the process of re-inventing education should be focused upon the ultimate purpose of life: for the human heart to achieve the same quality of love as the Creator's heart. That is the only path to permanent peace. Let us nurture that heart most carefully from its beginning through its maturity. As young adults with such heart are infused into this chaotic world, the raging seas of iniquity will be calmed and we will begin to see the true potential of humanity on the horizon.

Appendix:

- Information about Rev. Dr. Sun Myung Moon: http://

www.reverendsunmyungmoon.org/

- Searchable text of Rev. Dr. Sun Myung Moon's sermons: http://unification.net/
- An example of interactive online classrooms: http://www.interactiveonlineclassroom.com/aboutus/
- Statistics on school crime in America: http://www.ncvc.org/ncvc/main.aspx?dbName= Document Viewer & Document ID=32368
- Examples of school shootings throughout the world: http://www.infoplease.com/ipa/A0777958.html
- Article about cheating on tests in South Korea: http://www.asiaone.com/News/Latest%2BNews/Asia/Story/A1Story20100125-194334.html
- A book on the topic of the decline of education in America: http://search.barnesandnoble.com/American-Higher-Education-in-Decline/Kenneth-H-Ashworth/e/9780890969731
- The U.N. resolution about the importance of youth for peace: http://www.un-documents.net/a40r14.htm

*****

Part 5
Case Studies

1

Globalization and Multiculturalism as Paradigm Shifts in Higher Education: The Role of the Trakya University in Sustaining Academic, Social and Cultural Developments in the Balkans

Enver Duran, Fatma Özkan, Sema Duran and Aslı Özen

Abstract: Higher Education Institutions are the most important points of contact between the national and the international environments. Their global networks establish a platform for cooperation among nations and their citizens. Higher education has now become central to the changes due to the fact that worldwide networking and exchange are reshaping social, economic and cultural life. Higher education systems and policies are being transformed by globalization and multiculturalism. Thus, it can be argued that higher education institutions go through a paradigm shift which is urged to support the new formations of higher education institutions. The Trakya

University is aware of this shift and necessities trying to accomplish new dimensions within the context of globalization and multiculturalism. Being a regional institution, the Trakya University plays a significant role in the Balkans offering a wide range of global academic opportunities to the region and Balkans such as exchange and mobility programs, academic, social and cultural cooperation projects, foreign language education, internship trainings and leadership for social and cultural organizations. Creating such a cooperative environment in the Balkans it is also expected to be competent in the global competitiveness. In the frame of this paradigm shift regarding social and cultural values, globalization and multiculturalism has become one of the significant themes of educational trends. In this respect, the study aims to discuss the process of globalization and multiculturalism as a paradigm shift in Higher Education; more specifically, the role of the Trakya University in the Balkans.

Introduction

Globalization as a new paradigm for higher education policy became popular by the end of the last century and the beginning of the new millennium. The 1990s became an era of managerial restructuring and closure for some departments, faculties and institutions especially as the spectacular growth in participation experienced in the last few decades forced institutions not only to compete with each other in the market for student places but also absorb the cost of providing extra, unfunded student places, at declining levels of state funding. In the Twenty-First Century the university is becoming different institutions, one that is no longer linked to the destiny of the nation-state by virtue of its role as producer, protector and inculcator of an idea of national culture.

Globalization and Higher Education

Nowadays, international contexts have to be taken into account when higher education in developing countries has begun to integrate into the world community to meet with the global demands and even conform to the international practice. As the globalization process is transforming higher education across the world, and is expected to strongly influence the international nature of the university [Kishun, 1998:64], the concept of globalization has indeed become increasingly important to debates about the future of higher education, and educators need to examine the forces of globalization, the immediate background against which higher education internationalization is implemented in developing countries. It is thus high time to analyze the nature of globalization and how it affects higher education. A good understanding of these issues can perform a valuable service to bring a critical voice to the idea of globalization, which is all too often simply accepted as a positive force. [Yang, 2002]

Globalization means that national borders do not limit a nation's investment, production, and innovation. Two of the main bases of globalization are information and innovation, and they, in turn, are highly knowledge intensive. Why does globalization increase the demand for education and for educational quality? The answer lies in two parts. The first is economic: rising payoffs to higher education in a global, science-based, knowledge intensive economy makes the university training more of a *necessity* to get *good* jobs. The second part is socio-political: demographics [the changing family] and democratic ideals increase pressure on universities to provide access to groups that traditionally have not attended university. [Carnoy, 2005]

Multiculturalism and Higher Education

Culture can be described as totality of thought processes, belief systems and behavioural patterns of a community, handed over to them by previous generations. Culture is community specific; it is the peculiarities of the people, who have developed a worldview according to their needs, their modes of living shaped by their geographical and social environments. Language, like culture, is community specific and is intricately interwoven with the culture it represents. Language helps members of the community to establish, assert and maintain their identity as individuals and as a group, bringing among them a sense of solidarity. ***"Communication is not passing of information, but involves conceptualization of concepts and experiences, of identification and classification, of argumentation and assertion through correct language."*** [Pattanayak DP, 1987] Communication is an important means of self-identification: our sense of identity is bound up with the culture and education.

Multiculturalism is the acceptance or promotion of multiple ethnic cultures. The idea behind multiculturalism is that multiculturalists advocate extending equitable status to distinct ethic and religious groups without promoting any specific ethnic, religious and cultural community values as the central. The term *multiculturalism* deeply impacts the academic discourse and the practice of comparative and international education.

Paradigm Shift in Higher Education

As noted in *the UNESCO World Education Report: Teachers and Teaching in a Changing World* [UNESCO, 1998], the young generation is entering a world, which is changing in all spheres: scientific and technological, political, economic, social and cultural. According to Cheng [1999], humans in the social context of the new millennium will be multiple, as technological persons, economic persons, social persons, political persons, cultural persons, and learning persons in a global village of information, high technology, and multi-cultures. Both individuals and the society therefore need multiple developments in technological, economic, social, political, cultural, and learning respects. Life-long learning and the learning society are necessary to sustain the continuous multiple developments of individuals and the society in a changing new century. [Drucker, 1995] To prepare our younger generation to meet the challenges of an ever advancing knowledge-based society and the dynamically changing environment, it is not enough to impart them with mere knowledge. Instead of teaching and learning huge volumes of information and factual materials, the content of education should put emphasis on developing students' abilities to *learn how to learn* systematically, creatively, and critically. We have to help them develop a global outlook, and equip them with a repertoire of skills and positive attitudes to respect knowledge and to learn how to learn.

According to Cheng [1999-2000], the paradigm in education should be shifted from the traditional school-bound one to a new triplication paradigm. The new paradigm emphasizes the development of students' contextualized multiple intelligences [CMI] [including technological, economic, social, political, cultural, and learning intelligences], and the processes of triplication [including globalization, localization, and individualization] in education. Given that societal and global contexts are so complicated, diverse, multiple, fluid, and challenging, it is quite reasonable to expect that the new generations should have at least some of the contextualized multiple intelligences to meet diverse challenges in the new millennium. Therefore, our education should be reformed with clear relevance and concrete linkages with the development of CMI.

Mobility

The result of globalization in country, mobility in higher education has modified Higher Education Institutions by integrating training in multiple modes of transportation to provide internal and external mobility.

Internal mobility in higher education, once recruited in higher education institutions, young teacher and researchers may benefit from different careers. People who do not climb the first step have very little chance of reaching higher levels. [ILO, 2000] Promotion is a main issue that individuals consider before entering into any profession. On the other hand it can be said that for the external mobility; acceptance and appreciation of diversity, greater international understanding, improved quality of learning and access to programs unavailable, improved capacity to work internationally, enriched life experience and networks for the future, prestige of foreign credentials. [Polak, 2009]

Student and staff mobility creates complex international groups who, in this case too, become a unique and temporary social group, which has an impact on the host university. And then, months later, they return to their place of origin, changed in various ways, and bringing change to their own university. Changes are of both kinds: hidden and evident, some easy to measure and document but many also impossible to capture in their complexity.

"Academic mobility in higher education, it is a commonplace to note, is an old, not a new phenomenon. It is an old phenomenon because the idea of a university is of a place of teaching and learning open to all, whatever their provenance, provided they can benefit themselves and others; and universities date back hundreds of years. In principle there is no limitation and universities are and have always been international institutions in their composition, but the fact that, despite their international character, universities today are de facto national institutions is mainly a function of the way they have been financed. Since what students can afford to pay is far less than the funds needed, in contemporary universities, for teaching, administration and, above all, for research, universities have had to be partially financed by the state, in the majority of cases and in most countries. The effect in the Twentieth Century was for universities to become national and the student body to be almost exclusively drawn from citizens of the state which was funding them. In the Twenty-First Century, when some states can no longer afford to finance universities for their full budget needs, students from other countries,

and the fees they bring, are becoming a 'natural' part of the student body. In some countries increasing numbers of self-funding, 'private' universities are more than willing to take students from any country. Whether financially motivated or not, universities are, once again, places where students-and staff, but for different reasons-hail from many nationalities, and finance is almost everywhere a major factor in student mobility." [Byram, Dervin, 2008]

Thanks to mobility, the concept of multiculturalism was born in countries. Intercultural adaptation and cooperation gain importance in multicultural countries. As subcultures' level of social adaptation increases, it becomes easier to maintain their cultural existence and development.

The Role of the Trakya University

The Trakya University [TU] provides consulting and coordination services in the international platform in cooperation with the University's academic and administrative units. It supports the idea of forming an intellectual environment, which is motivating the students, lecturers and sharers for the development in an international status. By considering the rapid changes in the Twenty-First Century, the aim of the TU is to widen education and train more students of a wider age group. Considering the needs of the region it increases the diversity and content of the curricula, provides the ease of employment by concentrating on practical training and foreign language training in order to sustain the academic development.

The TU is a member of the European University Association

[EUA], the International Association of Universities [IAU] and the Balkan Universities Union, and other international organizations and carries out tasks in order to conduct studies in the international arena with the sub-units of Erasmus, Farabi and Projects and International Relations that provide mobility.

As a member of the BUA [Balkan Universities Association], the TU has had a major role in developing the relationships between the Balkan Universities. In addition, other international associations, which the TU is a member of, include the EUA [European University Association] and the IAU [International Association of Universities]. Therefore, the basic elements of the TU's vision consist of having new partnerships to the universities in the other regions of the world, increasing the numbers of national and international exchange programmes, the participants to these programmes and projects carried out by the academic staff within the context of the LLP/Erasmus, Farabi and Leonardo da Vinci.

Mobility Programmes

Erasmus Exchange Programme

The Erasmus Programme is a European Union [the EU] student exchange programme established in 1987. It forms a major part of the EU Lifelong Learning Programme 2007-13, and is the operational framework for the European Commission's initiatives in higher education.

Erasmus Programme has been active under the authority of International Relations Office Erasmus Coordinator-ship, the TU since April, 2004. The National Agency [NA] is responsible for controlling and counseling the Erasmus activities of all the universities in Turkey and the TU has been working in cooperation with the National Agency since 2004.

The TU considers internalization to be a great importance to be integrated in the European Higher Education Area and the European Research Area. The TU's objectives concerning Erasmus activities are focusing on both qualitative and quantitative improvement of student and staff mobility, implementation of European Credit Transfer System [the ECTS] effectively within the university in accordance with curricular reform, and engaging in more the IP and Multilateral Projects.

Actions under Erasmus Programme run by the TU are: Student Mobility [SM]; Student Mobility for Studies [SMS], Student Mobility for Placements [SMP]; and the Staff Mobility [ST]; Staff Mobility for Teaching Activities [STA], and Staff Mobility for Training [STT].

Erasmus Bilateral Agreement

In 2009-10 academic year the TU has **57** bilateral agreements with **43** universities in **15** different European Union countries, which include Austria, Germany, Belgium, Bulgaria, Czech Republic, Denmark, Finland, The Netherlands, England, Spain, Italy, Hungary, Poland, Slovenia and Greece. The following table shows the numbers of participants in Erasmus Exchange Program according to the years:

[For 2010-11 academic year only outgoing students have been selected. Through the following year, other staffs and students are going to be selected]

Years	Student Mobility		Staff Mobility	
	Outgoing	Incoming	Outgoing	Incoming
2004-2005	7	—	2	—
2005-2006	18	—	10	3
2006-2007	13	1	3	1
2007-2008	25	8	6	5
2008-2009	30	9	—	6
2009-2010	40	22	8	5
2010-2011	77	?	?	?
TOTAL	**210**	**40**	**29**	**20**

Farabi Exchange Programme

The International Exchange Programme of Students and Faculty Members between Higher Education Institutions, in short *Farabi* is an Exchange programme of students and faculty members between higher education institutions, which give education at associate degree, undergraduate, graduate and doctorate levels within the scope of universities and higher technology institutes. The Farabi Exchange Programme aims that students or faculty members continue their education and teaching activities at a higher education institution other than their own for one or two semester [s].

The principles regarding the application of the Farabi Exchange Programme have been determined in detail by Regulations, Principles and Procedures. ***"Regulation Regarding Student and Faculty Member Exchange Program between Higher Education Institutions"*** became effective after being published in the Official Gazette of February 18 , 2009 and numbered 27145. Financial principles of the Farabi Exchange Program are issued according to ***"Principles and Procedures Regarding the Usage and Recognition of the Amount to be Transferred to Higher Education Institutions, Payments within This Context, and Other Matters by the Higher Education Board with the Purpose of Supporting Student and Faculty Member Exchange Programmes between Higher Education Institutions."***

The Farabi Exchange Programme has been carried out by the TU since 2009. The TU has the Farabi Exchange Protocols with thirty-five state universities and one Foundation University within the scope of the Farabi Exchange Programme as of January 1, 2010.

Contribution of the Trakya University to Academic, Cultural and Social Development of the Universities in the Balkans

Academic Cooperation

International cooperation has strongly intensified during the last decades owing to rapid developments in scientific communication. Economic, political and intra-scientific factors also influence international collaboration links among individual countries.

The TU has cooperation agreements with fifty-nine universities from twelve countries. It aims to create academic and research network under the frame of these protocols by establishing university environment, which have a stimulating effect on connecting especially Balkan nations and cultures in an academic sphere. This network becomes stronger and effective through joint academic conferences and scientific projects, student and academic exchanges, the exchange of publications and materials of common interest, research collaboration, summer schools, training and internship programmes.

Balkan Countries Librarians Union

The Balkan Countries Librarians Union that was established on July 29, 2009 by gathering representatives from the Balkan libraries has a significant role for the exchange of publications and materials of common interest in Balkans. The TU, having cooperation protocols with forty-two Balkan University Libraries, has needed to carry out studies in the field of librarianship and information science in parallel with the mission and vision undertaken. To meet this need, as a result of the evaluation charter declared after *"The Balkan Countries' Inter Library Information-Document Management and Collaboration."* Evaluation Symposium held by the TU, the union has been established. The union has three separate goals: to increase the professional communication and cooperation between libraries in the Balkans, to digitalize scientific studies by compiling them and create open archives, and to digitalize and share the common cultural heritage of the Balkans by exposing it.

Balkan Language Centre

As the TU is the regional university in the Balkans, it bases its international relations on this ground. The Department of Balkan Languages was established in 2007 in order to teach

Bulgarian Language and Literature, Greek Language and Literature, Albanian Language and Literature, Bosnian Language and Literature. The department has nearly 200 students. Romanian Language and Literature and Russian Language and Literature departments have also been opened and will become active with the demands of the students. Croatian Language and Literature Department was opened and has it been giving education to its students since 2009-10 academic year.

Balkan Application and Research Centre

The *Balkan Application and Research Centre* was founded in 2004 with the purposes of searching the mutual history, artistic and cultural values of Balkan countries; their social, political and economic similarities; cooperating with public, private institutions and corporations inside and outside Turkey; to follow and encourage team work; to lead and coordinate the academic cooperation with the Balkan Universities; to serve the values and culture of Turkey in the Balkans; to arrange conferences, seminars and boards; to announce the results via articles, magazines and books to public opinion both inside and outside Turkey.

Turkey-Bulgaria Meeting Point

The Turkey-Bulgaria Meeting Point, which contains selections of Bulgarian Literature, course books and a variety of materials was opened in 2009. The Meeting Point is a junction for the cultural centre between the Central TU and Bulgaria and the Balkans. It promotes the cultural values and offers opportunities to the students to develop their foreign language.

Summer School and Internship Training Opportunities

The TU offers the students studying Turkish Language and Literature at Universities in the Balkans Summer School Programmes in the Department of Turkish Language and Literature, Faculty of Letters. The students are involved in educational and cultural exchange activities as well as improve their second language. In the same way, the students studying Balkan Languages at the TU attend the Summer School Programmes offered by the Universities in the Balkans under the frame of Academic Protocols between the two universities. They get benefit from these kinds of programs in terms of both cultural and academic developments.

Furthermore, the TU offers internship trainings to the interns and nurses from Kosovo in the TU Hospital. They are provided clinical service training experience in the related clinics, exceptional knowledge and work experience in the hospital. The TU renews its agreement every year in order to give the opportunity more interns and nurses to develop themselves in their profession. They stay in Turkey during their training for two months and turn back to their countries, and then other interns are assigned to attend the programme.

Recently Organized Conferences, Symposium and Meetings

By the sense of leadership, the TU encourages the participation of the educators from the Balkans to the conferences, social and cultural events that are organized by the departments and faculties of the university.

Becoming a tradition with the contributions of the

participant countries from the Balkans "*The 5th International Balkans Education and Science Convention*" was held by the TU, Faculty of Education; Trakia University, Faculty of Education Stara Zagora-Bulgaria and St. Cyril and Methodius University, Faculty of Education Skopje-Macedonia between the dates October 1 and 3, 2009. In the convention, important contributions have been made to the contemporary education and teaching problems with theoretical and applied studies, and a comparative, interdisciplinary approach has been put forward.

Besides the convention mentioned above, the TU has taken a leadership to organize many symposiums, conferences, other social and cultural activities such as Balkans Forum [in 2005 Edirne], Balkan Congress [in 2006 Edirne] and Information/ Documentation Management and Cooperation among the Libraries in Balkan Countries Symposium [2009].

Last but not least, the TU hosted most of the Rectors from the Balkan Universities and organized the greatest event called, ***"The Third Balkan Universities Network Meeting – Balkan Spring Educational Conference"*** on May 7-8, 2010. This event provided Universities in the Balkans to form a network, share their experiences in Higher Education in terms of academic cooperation and new collaborations.

Conclusion

The TU supports a new educational vision to be able to provide global society within an education that meets current needs and that can respond efficiently to contemporary demands and challenges for the Balkans. These are characterized by globalization and multiculturalism.

By offering a wide range of global academic opportunities to the region and Balkans such as exchange and mobility programmes, academic, social and cultural cooperation projects, foreign language education, internship trainings and leadership for social and cultural organizations the TU creates such a cooperative environment in the Balkans and thus sustaining the academic, social and cultural developments of the region. It demonstrates great responsibility and accountability in their development processes.

Bibliography:

- Byram, M. and Dervin, F. 2008. *Students, Staff and Academic Mobility in Higher Education.* Canada: Cambridge Scholars Publishing.
- Carnoy, M. 2005. *Globalization, Educational Trends and the Open Society.* OSI Education Conference on *Education and Open Society: A Critical Look at New Perspectives and Demands.*
- Cheng, YC. 1999. *Curriculum and Pedagogy in the New Century: Globalization, Localization and Individualization for Multiple Intelligences.* Keynote speech presented at the Fifth UNESCO-ACEID International Conference with the theme *Reforming Learning, Curriculum and Pedagogy: Innovative Visions for the New Century* on 13-16 December, 1999, Thailand.
- Drucker, PF. 1995. *Managing in a Time of Great Change.* Oxford [UK]: Butterworth Heinerman.
- ILO. 2000. *Changing Conditions of Higher Education Teaching Personnel.*
- Geneva Kishun, Roshen. 1998. *Internationalization in South Africa* [In Peter Scott's, Edited, *The Globalisation of Higher Education,* pp. 58-69. Buckingham: Open University Press.
- Pattanayak, DP. 1987. *Multilingualism and Mother Education.* Delhi [India]: Oxford University Press.

- Polak, EE. 2009, June 12. *Access and International Mobility in Higher Education*. [Presentation] Turkey: Süleyman Demirel University.
- UNESCO. 1998. *Teachers and Teaching in a Changing World: The UNESCO World Education Report.*
- Yang, Rui. 2002. *Third Delight: The Internationalization of Higher Education in China*. New York and London: Rutledge.

*****

2

The Context of Globalized and Multicultural Educational Programmes and Support Services: The Sample of the Trakya University

Hilmi Ibar, Handan Çelik, Sema Duran and Aslı Özen

Abstract: Globalization, which is both a process and a theory, provides perspectives on ways, in which education is being shaped by global processes. Influences of globalization are multi-dimensional having large social, economic, political and most significantly educational implications. In globalization, it is not simply the time of economic exchange, political agreement binding the nations and societies, but also the shared consciousness of being part of a global system. That consciousness is conveyed through most systematically through formal education, which has taken on more subtle shapes. The inexorable transformation of consciousness brought on by globalization alters the content and contours of education, as universities taken on increasingly important role in this process. Because of the above-mentioned significance of globalization, in the Trakya University, much of the focus on the role of education in globalization has been on conveying of knowledge within an international scope. Therefore, in the context of globalization, many mobility activities are carried out some of which include Erasmus Exchange Programme under the *Lifelong Learning Programme*, the *Foreign National Students Exam* [YÖS], the *Bologna Process*, the *Training Education and Consultancy and Internship Services*, which help to make academic degree and quality assurance standards more compatible throughout Europe. Through these programs, multiculturalism and collaboration between universities are encouraged as improving the quality of education and increasing the amount of multilateral cooperation between higher education institutions both in the Balkans and Europe by spreading new pedagogic practice constitutes one of the main purposes of the Trakya University to achieve globalization, and thus multiculturalism in education. This includes the fundamental right of all learners, that is: the promotion of understanding and tolerance in education and it is provided through globalization. Therefore, peace education in addition to multicultural education via different facilities stated above within the scope of globalization is an inseparable part of basic quality education of the Trakya University. In this study it is aimed to present the sample of the Trakya University within the context of globalized and multicultural educational programs and support services.

Introduction

Education policies, which have long existed as a part of appropriate and good quality human resource development played an important role in development policy in general. Education as stated by TeVelde [2005] as an important driver of growth and poverty reduction is central, directly and indirectly, to achieve development and globalization goals. Insights into appropriate policies for globalization and education and the importance of a balanced approach towards supporting services for all levels of education both in the Balkan and the European countries are addressed in this report.

Therefore, this study narrates the main links between globalization processes and education by discussing; the quantity and quality of education and training within the framework of whether and how the Trakya University participates in the processes of educational globalization with the Balkan and the European countries, how this participation process affect the demand and supply of education and training, and institutional policies attempted to reconcile the human resource development and the processes of globalization in order to obtain the maximum impact.

Globalization of Education at the Trakya University

In a globalized society education plays a vital role for bringing any changes or modifications, which are mostly caused for and welcomed by a majority of the learners across countries. So, *borderless education* as cited by Sethy [2008] is one of the most visible evidences of globalization. The increase both in the neighbor Balkan countries and European Countries is one of the reasons to trend the learners to get the opportunity in the globalized world via the *Erasmus Exchange Programme* under the *Lifelong Learning Programme*, the *Foreign National Students Exam* [YÖS], the *Bologna Process*, the

Training Education and Consultancy and Internship Service facilities at the Trakya University. These facilities create an environment where most of the learners both inside and outside the mentioned countries access the quality education through cooperation and collaboration. Because, the Trakya University, as a member of the *European Universities Union, the International University Union* and other international organizations, provides consulting and coordination services in the international platform in cooperation with the University's academic and administrative units. Additionally, the TU carries out tasks in order to conduct studies in the international arena with the sub-units of Erasmus, National and International Projects and International Relations that provide mobility.

In this respect, international scope is totally integrated into the education system of the Trakya University by means of various services as mentioned above, to meet the new demands being created by globalization. Thus, the aim of the existing educational system of the Trakya University is to provide training opportunities for learners and academicians who are both in pre and in-service stage. Some of these facilities include pedagogical teacher training or medical internship, in addition to the basic exchange programs available via the *Erasmus Exchange Programme* or the *Foreign National Students Exam.*

Therefore, to meet the challenges of globalization, it would in fact appear necessary to prepare individuals for a workplace where responsibilities are constantly changing, where management is replaced by networking, that is one of the education policies of the Trakya University, where information passes through multiple and informal channels, where initiative-taking is more important than obedience, and strategies are especially complex because of the educational and training expansion beyond national borders. So, in regard to education, the aim is to deliver more and better cross-national and cross-cultural education by means of the incorporation.

In addition to these, the Trakya University aims to harmonize the academic units with the *European Higher Education Area and European Research Area* by developing and popularizing the studies of mobility programmes, establishing a balance between diversity and unity targeted at the *European Higher Education Area*, conducting project programmes aimed at regional development and the improvement of cross-border cooperation, conducting the total country-based activities envisaged for the *Lifelong Learning Programme* within the framework of the agreement to be signed by Prime Ministry and the *European Commission*, and in this context, conducting studies about providing active participation from the academic staff and students to the activities, which will be carried out within the framework of the *Lifelong Action Plan*, that is the *Lifelong Learning Strategy Document.*

As having been working for the establishment of the BUA [the Balkan Universities Association], the Trakya University has had a major role in developing the relationships between the Balkan Universities. In addition, other international associations, in which the Trakya University is a member, include the EUA [the Europe Universities Association] and the IAU [the International Association of Universities]. Therefore, the basic elements of the Trakya University's vision consist of having new partnerships to the universities in the other regions of the world, increasing the numbers of national and international exchange programmes, the participants to these programmes and projects carried out by the academic staff within the context of LLP/Erasmus, *Farabi and Leonardo da Vinci*.

Here, the profound implications of globalization for education is drawn out, which are all formally delivered through cross-universities cooperation to encourage both the mutual benefit and development of the academicians and students between the higher education institutions in the Balkan countries as much as the European ones. However, the significance of the cultural similarities shared by most of the countries taking place in the Balkans cannot be underestimated such as the languages or the cross-national interest in each other's culture, which encourages the establishment of mutual cooperation between the Trakya University and most of the Balkan Universities.

Lifelong Learning Programme

In recent years, conventional understanding has left its place to a modern, developing and information society because of the development of the technology and internet that covers our life. People need to develop themselves to survive and to adjust to life. To fulfill this aim, life-long learning concept that has an important place especially in Europe begins to have importance in our country needs to be examined with its different qualifications.

"Lifelong learning is the development of human potential through a continuously supportive process

which stimulates and empowers individuals to acquire all the knowledge, values, skills, and understanding they will require throughout their lifetimes and to apply them with confidence, creativity and enjoyment in all roles, circumstances, and environments." [Longworth and Davies, page 22]

This definition includes several basic elements of the lifelong learning ideal:

1. A belief in the idea of lifetime human potential and the possibility of its realization;
2. Efforts to facilitate achievement of the skills, knowledge, and aptitudes necessary for a successful life;
3. Recognition that learning takes place in many modes and places, including formal educational institutions and non-formal experiences such as employment, military service, and civic participation and informal self-initiated activity; and
4. The need to provide integrated supportive systems adapted to individual differences that encourage and facilitate individuals to achieve mastery and self-direction. Society should make these systems available to learners with flexibility and diversity.

Education and training development may be based on many geographical areas other than countries. National and regional governments tend to have the best overview of systems, and might seem to be best placed to initiate broad policy changes. Educational institutions, community-based organizations and companies serve areas which may be smaller than, larger than or overlapping with a country. The concept of life-long learning's origin has based on the period of time in Europe. The educational studies in Europe, which have developed under the lifelong learning concept, have reported at the *UNESCO*, the *OECD* and the *EURYDICE*. However, this concept has recently started to be awarded in Turkey and we have developed studies dealing with this issue to give greater encouragement to its uptake.

The reform carried out in the context of the *Bologna process* in 2008 led to the creation of a national qualifications framework aimed at improving the recognition of professional qualifications and extending access to higher education. Because as stated by Marginson and Der Wende [2006], the *Bologna Process* together with the *Lisbon Strategy* are the main vehicles or frameworks guiding the European response to globalization in higher education. An agency was established in 2008 to manage qualification procedures such as licensing, accreditation and assessment. The national qualifications system is to be linked to the existing European framework.

The Varied Nature of Educational Access at the Trakya University

We now come to examine the varied nature of educational access between the Trakya University and the Universities among which various cooperation agreements have been available for the promotion of mutual benefit and improvement.

In many cases, the educational expansion between these higher education institutes satisfies the demand for mobility and thus the flexibility, and has made it imperative to develop more flexible approaches to cooperate between higher education institutes.

Let us take as an example, the mobility programmes between the Trakya University and the Balkan and some of the European countries.

Mobility Programmes via the Trakya University Support and Their Results

A. Erasmus Exchange Programme

The Erasmus Programme [European Region Action Scheme for the Mobility of University Students] is a European Union [the EU] student exchange programme established in 1987. It forms a major part of the *EU Lifelong Learning Programme 2007–2013*, and is the operational framework for the European Commission's initiatives in higher education.

Erasmus named after a Dutch humanist and theologian, Erasmus of Rotterdam [1466 – 1536], is the European Commission's programme for Higher Education and HE/FE students, teachers and institutions. It was introduced in 1987 with the aim of increasing student mobility within the European Community, subsequently including the *European Economic Area* countries and the Candidate Country of Turkey. In 1995 Erasmus was incorporated into the Socrates programme, which supported the European dimension in education from school, to university, and through adult life [BCL]. The Socrates Programme ended on December 31, 1999 and was replaced with the *Socrates II Programme* on January 24, 2000, which in turn was replaced by the *Lifelong Learning Programme 2007–2013* on January 1, 2007.

Erasmus Programme has been active under the authority of the *International Relations Office Erasmus Coordinatorship*, the Trakya University since April, 2004 after applying the *European Commission* and getting the *Erasmus University Charter*, which has been renewed in 2007 [according to the senate decision number 18 from the meeting dated 26.01.2007] the *National Agency* [the NA] is responsible for controlling and counselling the Erasmus activities of all the universities in Turkey and Trakya University has been working in cooperation with the National Agency since 2004.

The Trakya University [TU] considers internalization as of great importance to be integrated in the *European Higher Education Area* and the *European Research Area*. The Trakya University's objectives concerning Erasmus activities are focusing on both qualitative and quantitative improvement of student and staff mobility, implementation of the *ECTS Credit System* effectively within the university in accordance with curricular reform, and engaging in more IP and Multilateral Projects.

The strategies to realize these objectives are to:

- Provide all the Trakya University members with detailed information and analysis of changes happening within the Erasmus Programme resulting from the LLP;
- Update the *ECTS Course Catalogue Database* at our official web-site continuously;
- Initiate teaching staff for organizing multilateral and the IP projects to be offered firstly to our present partners; and

- Promote Erasmus programme through our *EU Link* at our official web-site, regular student and teaching staff meetings.

Actions under the *Erasmus Programme* run by the Trakya University International Relations Erasmus Office are: the Student Mobility [the SM]; the Student Mobility for Studies [the SMS], the Student Mobility for Placements [the SMP] and the Staff Mobility [the ST]; the Staff Mobility for Teaching Activities [the STA], the Staff Mobility for Training [the STT]. The following tables show the exchange numbers of the mobilities:

Table 1: The number of outgoing students between the years 2004-2005

Greece	Bulgaria	Italy	Hungary	Germany	Poland	France	England	Spain
6	8	4	43	48	11	5	5	3

Table 2: The number of incoming students between the years 2004-2005

Greece	Bulgaria	Poland	Hungary	Czech Republic
10	26	1	2	1

Table 3: The Outgoing Staff Mobility for Teaching Activities [STA]

Greece	Italy	Finland	Germany	Hungary	Spain	Bulgaria	Slovenia	Netherlands	Belgium
10	1	1	3	9	2	5	1	1	1

Table 4: The Incoming Staff Mobility for Teaching Activities [STA]

Greece	Bulgaria	Germany	Italy	Slovenia
3	14	1	1	1

B. Erasmus Bilateral Agreements

In 2009-2010 academic year, the Trakya University International Relations Office Erasmus Exchange Programme Coordinatorship has 57 bilateral agreements with 43 universities in 15 different European Union countries including; Austria, Germany, Belgium, Bulgaria, Czech Republic, Denmark,

Finland, The Netherlands, England, Spain, Italy, Hungary, Poland, Slovenia and Greece. The following table shows the exchange numbers of the mobility in accordance with the previous or current bilateral agreements.

Table 5: The Exchange Number of Mobilities

Years	Student Mobility		Staff Mobility	
	Outgoing	Incoming	Outgoing	Incoming
2004-2005	7	—	2	—
2005-2006	18	—	10	3
2006-2007	13	1	3	1
2007-2008	25	8	6	5
2008-2009	30	9	—	6
2009-2010	40	22	8	5
TOTAL	133	40	29	20

Foreign National Student Exam [YÖS]

Foreign National Student Exam, referred to as YÖS, has been designed for foreign students wishing to study in Higher Education Institutions in Turkey and on the results of this examination they can apply to the *Turkish Institutions of Higher Education.*

This examination is prepared and administered by the *Student Selection and Placement Centre* [the ÖSYM]. Applicants must hold the nationality of a country other than the Republic of Turkey or the Turkish Republic of Northern Cyprus. Applications will not be accepted from persons with Dual Nationality rights, one of which is for the countries named above. The applicants must have completed or be in their final year of secondary education in a school in which the education is equivalent to that of a Turkish Lyceée.

Within the framework of both a globalized and multicultural educational setting, in 2009, the TU has also placed students with reference to the *Foreign National Education Exam* [the YÖS] from various Balkan countries to a wide range of departments including Medical Sciences, Engineering and Architecture, Teaching, Applied Sciences.

Conclusion

Therefore, the Trakya University, which serves for globalized education may represent for a community of particular culture in a multicultural setting consisting of learners from diverse nations, also represents new definitions of multiculturalism.

All the educational facilities which accordingly led to the interaction of the culture between the cooperated countries can be also regarded as the product and producer of educational globalization. All of these programs conclude in educational access, with a combination in the wider context of globalization showing that it forces deeply and in various ways the educational and cultural collaboration of the Universities that are expected to do so more drastically in the future.

Bibliography:

- Marginson and Der Wende. 2006. *Globalisation and Higher Education.* Prepared for OECD.
- Longworth, N and Davies, WK 1996. *Lifelong Learning: New Vision, New Implications, New Roles for People, Organizations, Nations and Communities in the Twenty-First Century.* London [UK]: Kogan.

- Sethy, SS. 2008. *Distance Education in the Age of Globalization: An Overwhelming Desire Towards Blended Learning.* TOJDE: Turkish Online Journal of Distance Education-No. 9 [3], 29-44
- TeVelde, DW. 2005. *Globalization and Education: What do the Trade, Investment and Migration Literatures Tell Us?* Westminster Bridge Road, London's Overseas Development Institute: Working Paper 254

*****

Index

[S]

[T]

*****